Presented to:

_____

From:

_____

Date:

_____

365 Devotions for Living Joyfully

365 Devotions for Living Joyfully

Copyright © 2017 by Zondervan

Requests for information should be addressed to:

Zondervan, 3900 Sparks Dr., SE, Grand Rapids, MI 49546

ISBN 978-0-310-08550-8

Cover design: Kathy Mitchell

Interior design: Lori Lynch

Printed in China

22 23 24 25 26 /GRI/ 10 9 8 7 6 5 4 3

JANUARY

Pressing Toward the Goal

I press on toward the goal to win the prize for which God has called me heavenward in Christ Jesus.

—Philippians 3:14

Setting a goal is an honorable thing to do, but discouragement can set in quickly if the goal can't be realized until the distant future. To keep your joy as you press toward your target, pay close attention to the positives that happen *immediately* . . . and then a week or a month down the road. Keep a journal; take note of every improvement, no matter how trivial it seems. For example, if your goal is to lose thirty pounds, don't record just weight but also the many other changes that happen: Are you sleeping better at night? Are your moods more stable? Have you had more energy for tasks like mowing the yard? Have you been less depressed? Have you noticed changes in your hair or skin? Many people have set out to lose pounds only to discover myriad fringe benefits, such as improved posture, that had a shocking impact on their lives and their outlook on life.

Living joyfully means focusing on the goal *and* all the perks along the way.

Lord, I want every single thing You have for me as I press toward my goals. Help me to see and appreciate all the little benefits along the way.

The Joy of Setting Goals

May He grant the dreams of your heart and see your plans through to the end.

—Psalm 20:4 VOICE

A happy person has goals, both short-term and long-term. Smaller goals keep us motivated; as we reach them, we're reminded that we can, in fact, achieve worthwhile things. Bigger, long-term goals help us to focus beyond ourselves and our everyday routines. Goals should be well-defined to keep us on track—when we know where we're headed, we're less likely to say yes to projects that aren't meant for us. Finally, for the Christian, goals must always line up with God's will and Word, which will keep us from wandering away from Him.

If you don't have distinct goals, determine to set three in one or more of the following areas:

Relational (*designate one Girls' Day Out each month with your daughter*);

Emotional (*work with a counselor on anger issues once a week*);

Spiritual (*read through Isaiah within the next month*);

Health (*get your cholesterol down twenty points within 90 days*);

Creative (*take a watercolor class*); or

Intellectual/professional (*increase your productivity by 15 percent this quarter*).

Thank You for the grace to keep moving forward in my goals, Lord. May they always line up perfectly with Your will and call on my life.

So Little Time?

Don't imagine . . . that God's timetable is the same as ours . . . for
with the Lord, one day is like a thousand years, and a thousand
years is like one day.

—2 Peter 3:8 VOICE

People with many interests sometimes struggle with feeling overloaded or very short on time. As a result, they might also be oblivious to their many blessings. Maybe you're juggling a pottery class, volunteer work, and a full Crossfit regimen—not to mention three kids, a spouse, and a career. If so, you probably have little time left at the end of the week. *So let something go*, your spouse suggests, but if you love everything you're doing, it's easier said than done!

If you lack the time to do everything you want to do, count it all joy by remembering that the alternative is *satisfaction with the status quo*. As someone said, "People with many interests live not only longest but happiest." Those who keep their minds and bodies sharp by continuing to learn and develop are generally more joyful than those who take little interest in anything new.

And remember that, as the child of an infinite God, you have not just eighty years to explore life to the fullest, but an eternity.

Lord, thank You for making me curious about all the wonderful
things in the world and giving me time to pursue them!

God-Dreams

"Come, follow me," Jesus said.

—Matthew 4:19

few things will bring joy to your life like knowing you're following the dreams God has put in your heart. Even when the process is difficult, it's worth it just to know you're headed in the direction God has mapped out for you.

If you've lost your joy lately, make sure you haven't deviated from the path you're meant to travel. Sadly, we can spend precious time—sometimes even a lifetime—fulfilling someone else's dreams. This isn't to say you mustn't sacrifice your life for another: spending yourself caring for a sick child or mentally ill sibling, for example, might well be God's perfect will for you. It's not that life must be about you, but it must be about *God's will for you*. Giving in to someone's demands to help her reach her selfish goals isn't sacrificial; it's disobedient.

Are your current activities leading you toward the dreams God's given you or away from them? Determine today to know the joy of realizing your God-dreams by saying yes to His perfect plan for you.

Lord, if I've wandered off the path You laid out for me, set me straight. Thank You.

There's Got to Be More

Do not forget to rejoice, for hope is always just around the corner.
—Romans 12:12 VOICE

ountless people through the centuries have asked the same question: *Surely this isn't all there is. There's got to be more than this—right?*

For the unbeliever, there *is* only this life—eighty or so years in which to accomplish one's goals, create beauty, share love and kindness, and experience joy. Once the body dies, time's up, and then judgment.

But for the Christian there is definitely "more than this"—infinitely, astoundingly more. The day we finish this earthly life, we've only just begun. Then we embark on life in the fullest, spent face-to-face with God along with our heavenly family. Even during the most depressing, frustrating, or sorrowful day on earth, we have a light—not just any light, but the glorious Light Himself, at the end of the tunnel. We have a hope that only those who belong to Jesus have, and the joy that knowledge gives.

Lord, remind me on my difficult days that You're the Light at the end of my tunnel. Thank You that I know there's far, far more than this.

Answers

I call out to the LORD, and he answers me from his holy mountain.
—Psalm 3:4

sn't it almost overwhelming to think that God personally answers each of our prayers? Imagine how many administrators a political figure would have to hire to personally answer each and every letter from his or her constituents!

What false god can answer prayers? What false god is able to care for each of its worshipers personally, individually?

During any one of the wars involving America, letters to and from home were eagerly awaited and cherished. Sometimes an anxious mother or father would not hear from their beloved son or daughter for many days. When a letter finally arrived, they'd rejoice, and their home would once again be filled with joy. Likewise, when we call out to the Lord, praying for an answer, and that answer comes— even if it doesn't "say" exactly what we'd like to hear—we feel joy. Our God, Father of all humankind, answered *us*— personally and individually!

What a joy it is to know that when we call out to the Lord, He does answer. What a loving God!

Lord, it's so reassuring that when I reach out to You in prayer, I can know without a doubt that You'll answer. I thank You, Lord, and I accept Your answers.

Happy Place

You reveal the path of life to me; in Your presence is abundant joy; in Your right hand are eternal pleasures.

—Psalm 16:11 HCSB

Where's your happy place? Is it a coffee shop, a beachfront condo, or an old porch swing? Whether it's Grandma's kitchen, a quiet library, or a cabin in the woods, we all have places that make our hearts happy and lift our spirits.

The problem is that we can't always get to our happy places, can we? Family commitments, work responsibilities, and time constraints often prevent us from slipping away. Thankfully, there's something better than the earthly happiness that often seems just slightly out of reach.

As believers, we have a place of abundant joy that is always available and within reach, and that place is in the Lord's presence. Let's choose, each day, to remain near Him and bask in a joy that never waxes and wanes. We'll discover that, while happiness is dependent on our present circumstances, true joy is found in the presence of the One who loves us so.

Forgive me, Lord, for being satisfied with happiness when abundant joy is available to me. Help me live each day in Your presence.

Joy in the Reward

*"Blessed are you when people insult you, persecute you, and say
all kinds of evil against you because of me. Rejoice and be glad,
because great is your reward in heaven, for in the same way they
persecuted the prophets who were before you."*

—Matthew 5:11–12

Have you ever had someone turn his or her back on you because you stood for the Lord? Perhaps it was someone close to you who didn't understand or couldn't handle the things you were saying. Maybe the person had his or her own problems and the relationship just couldn't handle the stress. It's painful, isn't it?

Jesus knows a thing or two about the pain of broken relationships; He is very familiar with people persecuting, betraying, and abandoning Him. He also knows about the rewards of faithfulness and endurance. That's why He can tell His followers that we can "rejoice and be glad" no matter who ridicules us or turns us away.

While we don't enjoy the pain of the moment, we can be exceedingly glad knowing of the great reward to come. We can be filled with joy knowing that, in our suffering, we resemble our Savior. We can be gratified knowing that there is a great reward awaiting the faithful follower of Christ.

Give me the courage I need to stay the course, Lord. Help me to live like You lived, knowing a great reward is waiting.

Praying with Joy

In all my prayers for all of you, I always pray with joy.

—Philippians 1:4

If you grew up in church, you're familiar with prayer meetings. This is when prayer warriors gather to do business with the Lord. There's always that one individual who makes you long for just a portion of his or her passion.

It's clear, looking back, that prayers were so captivating because of the joy with which they were prayed. It wasn't the length of a prayer or the eloquence of the person that made even a teenager hang on to every word. It was the sense that the one praying counted it a privilege to pray and, therefore, was filled with joy when doing it.

Let's not fall into the habit of treating prayer like an item on our to-do list that falls somewhere between making the bed and checking the mail. Let's see prayer for what it is—an opportunity to be in the presence of the God who created everything and to talk with Him like a father or a friend. Doesn't that make you want to pray with a little more joy?

Lord, instill in me a passion and a joy for the privilege of prayer.

A Strong Core

We also pray that you will be strengthened with all his glorious
power so you will have all the endurance and patience you need.
May you be filled with joy.

—Colossians 1:11 NLT

These days we hear a lot about the importance of having a strong core, and for good reason. Your core is a collection of muscles that includes your abs as well as other muscles that are vital to movement. A solid core improves breathing, digestion, and cardiovascular health. It enables good balance and guards against injury. When you've got a strong core, situations that might cause injury to most people won't put you in traction or on crutches.

Joy in your inner core—that is, your soul and spirit, which influence every other part of who you are—ensures that you can handle many issues that life throws at you. You'll be far more able to deal with irritations and small crises; your mood won't swing crazily; you'll see things in relation to the big picture instead of equating every problem with disaster. Ask the Lord to make your inner core strong by granting you supernatural joy, and you'll find that your day-to-day life will become far more fulfilling.

I pray, Lord, that You'll give me a strong inner core, one of
supernatural joy, so that I can gracefully handle every circumstance.

Joy in the Mess

Godliness with contentment is great gain.

—1 Timothy 6:6

A common misconception is that the saying *Cleanliness is next to godliness* is straight out of the Bible. Cleanliness *is* a good thing, but next to godliness? Not necessarily. In fact, if we're too insistent on everything being "just so," we'll miss out on opportunities for joy.

Think about a few people whose cooking you adore. Chances are that at least one of them makes a grand mess while putting together a scrumptious meal. Some of the most skilled cooks are so "artistic" that they end up with butter on the cabinet or gravy on the floor every time they step into the kitchen. If you're the designated cleanup crew, you can respond in one of two ways when it's time to do dishes: *What a mess—how inconsiderate!* or *A meal like that was well worth a little butter on the cabinets.*

Sometimes we want the "gourmet meals" of life without the messes, but that's not always possible. When we realize it's no big deal if life gets a little sloppy, we'll find more joy in our circumstances.

Lord, help me to be more accepting of the messy parts of life so I don't miss out on the yummy parts.

Cast Your Cares

Cast your cares on the LORD and he will sustain you; he will never let the righteous be shaken.

—Psalm 55:22

Some of the most joyful people you will meet are fishermen. Imagine the scene for a moment: You're sitting on a cool, grassy bank somewhere. It's silent except for the sound of the water and an occasional bird singing. You have your fishing rod in your hand; you pull it back and cast your line. With all your might, you throw it forward and let it fly. You can hear the whiz of the line as it heads away and out of sight. It's pure joy.

This is the way the psalmist described releasing your cares. The word he used for *cast* can also be translated *hurl* or *fling*. In other words, pull your arm back, and, with all of your might, cast those cares as far away as you can. Watch as they disappear in the distance. Listen as they whiz out of sight. Then sit in silence knowing that the only thing you'll be reeling back in is joy.

The joy that accompanies the casting of our cares is immeasurable, Lord. Thank You for allowing me to cast my burdens onto You.

Joy of Sleep

In vain you rise early and stay up late, toiling for food to eat—for he grants sleep to those he loves.

—Psalm 127:2

Have you ever used the idiom *No rest for the weary*? It's used to describe a situation where a tired person must continue to work; that's the world's way. There's far more joy in Solomon's wisdom: sleep is a gift from our God.

Solomon was not referring to those who rise early to spend time in the Word or stay up late to spend time with family. The warning was to those of us who are caught up in anxious thoughts. We rise early and stay up late worrying about things we can't fix.

Do you know what the Lord wants you to do instead? He wants you to sleep. The Hebrew word here is *shenah* (shā nä) and it means, well, sleep. No hidden meanings; no alternative interpretations. If you're tired and drained of joy, the Lord gives you permission to go take a nap. Enjoy!

Thank You, Lord, for the gift of sleep. Teach me the wisdom in resting when I'm weary.

Let It Shine

This is why it is said: "Wake up, sleeper, rise from the dead, and Christ will shine on you."

—Ephesians 5:14

What wakes you up in the morning? Is it a morning jog, spending time in your Bible, or a hot cup of coffee on the front porch? For some, the key to waking up is to open all the window blinds. Nothing wakes them up and fills their hearts with joy quite like the sun shining on their faces!

Paul warned the Ephesians to not have anything to do with the works of darkness. People who live in the dark walk around as if half-asleep and do "fruitless deeds" (v. 11). If you have ever done something in secret that you wouldn't want others to know about, then you are very aware that there is no joy in living that way.

God invites us into the light so we can live with joy. But we have to wake up and choose to open the blinds of our hearts and let the Son shine on us. We have to turn our backs on the things of darkness (vv. 3–5) and choose the fruit of the light (v. 9), which includes a life of joy.

It's easy to be lulled to sleep by the things of this world, Lord. Awaken my spirit and let Your light shine on me.

Cattle on a Thousand Hills

For all the animals of the forest are mine, and I own the cattle on a thousand hills.

—Psalm 50:10 NLT

How often do you lose sleep because you're worried about finances? Maybe you're dealing with an unexpected bill or a job loss. Perhaps a need has arisen within the community to which you feel called to contribute, but you don't feel you have enough to give. When it comes to money, Satan wants us to either feel scared or stingy.

We can live joyfully no matter how much or little is in our bank account. The trick is to remind ourselves that it's all God's anyway. Understanding that God owns everything prevents two common worries.

First, knowing it's not ours prevents us from being stingy and being tempted to cling too tightly to money. Second, knowing everything is His prevents us from being scared because we're reminded that He's able to meet any need that comes our way.

Are you in need? Rejoice, because your God owns the cattle on a thousand hills.

Forgive me, Lord, for the times I've been stingy or fearful with my finances. I'll rejoice knowing it's all Yours.

In My Affliction

I will be glad and rejoice in your love, for you saw my affliction and knew the anguish of my soul.

—Psalm 31:7

aybe you've gone through a trying time and thought, *No one understands.* Have you ever felt invisible in your pain? The truth is that we'll all go through seasons where other people truly don't know how we feel. The trial seems more intense when we feel unnoticed and misunderstood.

Regardless of what friends or family recognize or don't, we can be glad and rejoice knowing that God sees us in the midst of our affliction. Not only does He see what's taking place, He's also very much aware of the condition of our souls. Nothing takes place in our lives without the watchful eye of our God seeing and taking note of it.

There's something about being seen (Genesis 16:13) and having our pain known (Psalm 56:8) that makes it all a little more bearable. It's the only way we're able to live joyfully in the midst of painful circumstances.

I can endure with joy, Lord, knowing that Your eye is always on me and my pain never goes unnoticed by You.

Dance in the Dust

Let those who dwell in the dust wake up and shout for joy.

—Isaiah 26:19

Sometimes we feel as frail as the dust from which we came. The hurts and heartaches of this world drive us to our knees, and for a moment the dirt of the earth is all we're able to recall. We make ourselves at home in the ashes, and everything seems suddenly fragile.

Yes, like Paul, we have those days when there seems to be no rest for body or spirit (2 Corinthians 7:5). Morning brings exhaustion, and evening brings affliction. Then ten little words change everything: "I can do everything through Christ, who gives me strength" (Philippians 4:13 NLT). Suddenly we're more than a people of the dust. We're a people who can rise up from the ashes and dance in the dust. No matter the trial or tragedy, we can say, "I can do everything."

Though we were formed in the dust, we also carry the God-breath inside of us. The world would have us broken, forever aware of our fragility, and fearful of ever rising again. But God desires much more for us. He calls to us through our pain and gives us permission to rise from the dust and shout for joy.

Lord, I won't lie defeated and discouraged in the dust. I'll rise, praise Your name, and shout for joy.

Afflicted

You, LORD, hear the desire of the afflicted; you encourage them, and you listen to their cry.

—Psalm 10:17

Are you having to endure affliction? Perhaps it's poverty, illness, abandonment, or anxiety. You are not alone! The Lord hears your cries for help, mercy, or a reprieve. Listen for His voice. He's promised to encourage you. He knows your heart, He understands your deepest desires. And He will answer.

Our God is the only CEO whose "office door" is always open. He never sleeps, never puts up a Do Not Disturb sign, and never leaves His post. Instead, He's always alert and always available. Unlike our friends, who might weary of hearing about our troubles, God wants us to take them to Him—again and again and again if necessary. So great is His love that He never tires of hearing from us. And no problem is too big—or too small—for Him to handle.

In your afflictions, turn confidently to the Lord, knowing that He's delighted to hear from you, and that He's able to solve any problem you might have. And then rejoice!

Lord, You're the great problem-solver. Help me to trust You with all my problems.

The Joy of a Clear Conscience

Direct my footsteps according to your word; let no sin rule over me.
—Psalm 119:133

One of the quickest ways to snuff out joy is to allow a "little" sin into your life—you know, the sort that's easy to ignore most of the time because it's nowhere near as serious as stealing or adultery, but it plagues you when things get quiet. You go about your business all day without giving it a second thought, but when you lie down at night—*bam*—there it is, nipping at your heels like a small but very annoying dog. You try to reclaim the joy you used to feel, but something's wrong. Your conscience has been sullied.

No one's ever been saved by being good enough to deserve salvation. But we're called to live in a way that pleases God, and when we do, we experience the joy that comes from a life of integrity. When we insist on our own way because it's fun, we feel the loss, and joy evaporates.

Determine today to never forfeit joy for temporary pleasure.

Lord, help me to boldly and bravely examine my conscience. I want to please You more than I want anything else.

The Joy of Letting Go

I will sing of Your strength and will joyfully proclaim Your faithful love in the morning. For You have been a stronghold for me.

—Psalm 59:16 HCSB

"I can do it!" bellows your toddler as you start digging a trench in the garden, so you seize the teachable moment and let her try, even though you know the job is too big for her. She's a determined one, often able to do what she sets her mind to do, but this time the chore is too much. Finally she asks you to help, and as you take the trowel from her hands, she relaxes, never giving it another thought.

Author Corrie ten Boom wrote about how to handle our own powerlessness: turn to the power of Jesus. We, like children, can relinquish control and relax into Jesus' ability when faced with an impossible task. We might still have to involve ourselves in the situation, but admitting our incompetence and placing it all in His hands will restore our joy.

If you've been banging your head against the wall, let Jesus take over your dilemma, and refuse to fret about it any longer. Be confident in His ability, and your joy will be renewed.

Jesus, right now I call on Your power to do what I can't do. I receive joy because I'm confident in Your ability.

Joyfully Patient

"As for that in the good soil, they are those who . . . bear fruit with patience."

—Luke 8:15 ESV

Patience always frees up room for joy. No one ever said, "I love lessons in patience!" but it's a discipline that should be learned, and most of us would agree that it produces good things.

Elisabeth Elliot once said that restlessness affects nothing but our joy and contentment. In other words, we can forfeit peace and joy by giving in to impatience, even though it's powerless to change a single thing. For example, imagine you're eager for a certain change to take place, such as a job promotion or retirement or college graduation, but you've got three months to wait until the dream becomes reality. Whether you spend those three months wringing your hands with impatience or good-naturedly making the best of your time, they won't expand *or* shrink one iota. Three months consists of roughly 131,500 minutes, no matter your attitude. You might as well spend the time calmly and joyfully. Your life will be far better for it.

You know the events and changes I'm looking forward to, Lord.
Help me to be joyfully patient so I don't miss this valuable lesson.

Hiddenness: A Blessing

For you died, and your life is now hidden with Christ in God.
—Colossians 3:3

ave you ever felt as if your efforts were overlooked and unappreciated? Maybe you dedicated multiple evenings and half a paycheck to make sure Vacation Bible School was a hit, but in the end no one realized you were responsible for pulling it off. Or maybe you're stretched so thin from raising small children that you don't have time to be involved in anything ambitious in the first place. Paul said of the years immediately after his conversion, "I did not go up to Jerusalem to see [the other apostles], but I went into Arabia. Later I returned to Damascus. Then after three years, I went up to Jerusalem" (Galatians 1:17–18). This period in Paul's life (about which we know very little) reminds us there are seasons of hiddenness. We're out of the public eye, and sometimes no one's around to applaud when we do well.

The hidden times were crucial to Paul being prepared to change the world, which is why he knew how to be joyful in all circumstances. Living joyfully means recognizing that hiddenness isn't a punishment; it's a blessing.

Lord, while I'm out of the public eye, prepare me for whatever the future holds, teach me patience, and help me be humble and content.

The Joy of Hiddenness

Jesus got up, left the house and went off to a solitary place, where he prayed.

—Mark 1:35

We all love stories about caterpillars that become butterflies after a season in the cocoon, or tiny seeds that sprout into saplings after spending the winter in the cold soil. If we're wise, we'll realize that a time of hiddenness is crucial to becoming who we're meant to be. Therefore, if you're experiencing such a time, make sure you're taking full advantage of it even though your efforts are currently for the Lord's eyes only. As you throw yourself into all you do for Him, ask yourself, *Am I willing to do my job with excellence even though my colleagues seem unaware of my contribution? Am I willing to sing for an audience of One? To pray even though no one knows I'm on my knees day after day?*

Today, if your life or ministry is hidden, surrender everything you do to the Lord. Let His approval be more than enough, and your joy will increase exponentially. Remember: this isn't wasted time! Rejoice in this season, and you're sure to look back on it with fondness.

Sometimes I fee invisible to everyone but You, Lord. So I acknowledge that everything I do is for Your eyes only until You bring me out of this season.

Kindness Breeds Joy

Therefore, as God's chosen people, holy and dearly loved, clothe yourselves with compassion, kindness, humility, gentleness and patience.

—Colossians 3:12

Some of the most surprising things can shift your day from "blah" to joyful—for example, doing something kind for someone who's not currently on your "favorite people" list. Has your husband been driving you crazy with a hundred annoying habits? Order a couple of tickets to a movie he's been wanting to see. Have you caught yourself feeling annoyed with a loved one? Surprise her with her favorite meal. Did the last visit from your in-laws leave you exasperated? Have a small houseplant delivered to their door with a note: "Just because."

Gestures like these take a little investment and time (and sometimes a lot of pride-swallowing), but they can radically change a sour attitude into an agreeable one. You'd think that the appropriate mood would need to *precede* an act of kindness, but many times it happens the other way around because kindness opens the way to other fruits of the Spirit, such as joy.

Lord, help me to have the humility to do something thoughtful for someone who needs a little kindness from me this week.

Focus on Today

"Therefore do not worry about tomorrow, for tomorrow will worry about itself. Each day has enough trouble of its own."

—Matthew 6:34

It's confession time: raise your hand if you're a worrier. If you're like many people, you raised your hand, so let's talk about it. Worry isn't a fruit of the Spirit. This means that, when we choose worry, we are saying, "No, thank You" to the Spirit's fruit, which happens to include joy. Let's be honest—no one sits around worrying about tomorrow with a heart full of joy. Worry and joy do not coexist.

Let's choose to live joyfully by choosing to focus on today. God is already handling tomorrow, next week, and next year. We don't have to worry about them. Through Christ, we have everything we need to handle *today* with peace, patience, and joy. When we pick up the burden of worrying about tomorrow, we are choosing to set aside the joy for today because we can't carry both.

Surely you would much rather have joy. Let's focus on the joys of today and trust God with the worries of tomorrow.

Forgive me, Lord, for the times I have chosen worldly worry over heavenly joy. Help me to keep my focus on the gift of today.

The Lord Is Kind

The LORD is righteous in all his ways and kind in all his works.
—Psalm 145:17 ESV

Have you ever been the recipient of someone else's random act of kindness? We can all agree that it feels pretty good. The person receiving the kindness is blessed, but the one being kind is equally blessed. Taking the time to be kind is one of the simplest ways to add joy to our lives.

We can know many things about God through His Word. He's faithful and forgiving. He's mighty and merciful. He's loving and long-suffering. Yet sometimes we forget that He's kind. The psalmist declared that His every work is one of kindness.

We miss out on joy when we fail to recognize the many kindnesses of the Lord. He didn't have to create waterfalls or beautiful, purple sunsets. He didn't have to make birds that sing and leaves that rustle. God's kind works are everywhere. We can live joyfully when we learn to see them.

Forgive me, Lord, for the times I've taken Your kindness for granted or failed to recognize it at all.

Rejoice and Do Good

I know that there is nothing better for people than to be happy and to do good while they live.

—Ecclesiastes 3:12

What's the best thing you can do with your life? According to the wisest man who ever lived, there's nothing better than to be joyful and to do good. The two are closely linked. Joyful people enjoy doing good, and doing good certainly brings joy to a person's heart.

Think about a good deed you've done. Whether it was babysitting someone's children, donating blood, or buying a stranger's meal, an act of kindness has a way of blessing the doer and the recipient alike. Paul encouraged the believers in Galatia to continue doing good (Galatians 6:9), and the author of Hebrews advised believers to spur one another on to good works (Hebrews 10:24).

A joyful heart is the natural by-product of seeking to do good for others. There is, as Solomon advised, nothing better. Do you need more joy? Look for ways to do good for someone today.

I'll honor You, Lord, by spending my days being joyful and doing good for my fellow people.

Layering

For everything that was written in the past was written to teach us, so that through the endurance taught in the Scriptures and the encouragement they provide we might have hope.

—Romans 15:4

ust as layering clothes in the winter helps protect your body against the ravages of the cold, "layering" the Word of God by daily Scripture reading will help protect your soul against the ravages of sin.

The most effective weapon we have to keep us from falling prey to the evil in the world and the temptations fired at us by Satan is the Word of God. Even Jesus, when He was tempted in the desert for forty days, used Scripture as His weapon (Matthew 4:1–11). The Bible itself reminds us numerous times to study the Scriptures. In Ephesians 6:11, we're told to "put on the full armor of God" in order to protect ourselves from "the devil's schemes"; and this armor includes the Word of God, the Bible.

If we're fully protected each day from the evil of the world and the schemes of the enemy, we'll have the fullness of joy.

Lord, I covenant with You that I'll read from the Bible each day. Thank You, Lord, that we have Your Word in writing!

Snowflake

We love because he first loved us.

—1 John 4:19

A photographer using homemade camera equipment photographs individual snowflakes. He uses various backgrounds and lighting to accentuate different details of the flakes. Together, the billions of snowflakes can form mountains of trouble, and the results can be some back-breaking jobs of shoveling, plowing, and pushing vehicles out of drifts—not to mention broken trees and caved-in roofs. But observed individually, each flake is a breathtaking object of incredible beauty.

We might see ourselves as just one of the billions of people walking the face of the earth, a virtually invisible smidgen in the mass that is humanity. God, however, sees each of us as a remarkably varied and beautiful individual, His own precious creation.

If you have any doubts about how much God loves you—personally and individually—think about this: Would God invest so much in a tiny snowflake that's here one moment and indistinguishable the next unless He'd invest at least as much time, love, energy, and creativity in you?

Dear God, thank You for investing so much of Yourself in creating me. I rejoice that You love me that much!

Gift of Joy

To the man who is pleasing in His sight, He gives wisdom, knowledge, and joy.

—Ecclesiastes 2:26 HCSB

Have you ever wondered how you could have just a portion of the joy that you see in certain people? If so, Scripture has good news for you. Joy doesn't go to the best or the brightest. You don't have to outwork and outlast all of the others. Joy is a gift from God to all those who are pleasing in His sight.

How can we be pleasing in His sight? Scripture tells us that all the Lord asks of us is that we do what is right, that we show mercy, and that we walk humbly with Him (Micah 6:8). That is what the Lord asks of us: justice, mercy, and humility. We are pleasing in His sight when we exhibit these qualities. Then He gives us wisdom, knowledge, and joy.

When we feel ourselves a little lacking in joy, let's ask God to reveal ways we can be pleasing in His sight.

Lord, open my eyes to opportunities to show justice, mercy, and humility as I go about my day.

Joy in Our Defender

You, LORD . . . listen to their cry, defending the fatherless and the oppressed.

—Psalm 10:17–18

Did you grow up without a father or mother? Have you had to suffer many trials, tribulations, and sorrows? Rejoice!

Why should you rejoice in the face of heartbreaking troubles? Because the Lord, your God, is your own faithful Defender. What more could you ask than to have the most powerful, tireless, and effective Advocate in the entire universe?

These words from Psalm 10 specify that God has a particularly warm spot in His great heart for the one who grew up without one or both parents, or who has suffered, or is even now suffering. God sees what we're going through. Don't forget, Jesus walked the earth as both fully God and fully man, and He felt every pain we experience. He knew physical pain, rejection, cold, heat, hunger, thirst, loneliness, frustration, torture—He experienced it all. Is it any wonder that He stands as our Advocate, ready to defend us and to bring justice? What joy we can take from that knowledge!

Thank You, Lord, for understanding what I'm feeling when I'm down. Thank You for loving me and defending me!

FEBRUARY

From Blues to Joy

He makes me lie down in green pastures. . . . He restores my soul.
—Psalm 23:2–3 ESV

Do you get the "winter blues"? Scientists say that the cold and often dreary weather of winter does indeed affect many people. If you're one of those who suffer mild depression in the winter months, never fear: spring will come! The trees and flowers—along with your joy—will blossom forth!

The trials and tribulations of life can and often do affect us in a similar way. Both the weather and life's trials can make us feel overwhelmed, lonely, and discouraged, which can result in the "blues." Remember, however, when trials strike you like winter blizzards, you can know that, in many thousands of years of winters, spring has never failed to come!

Psalm 23 tells us that God will make you "lie down in *green* pastures" (italics added), and there He'll "restore [your] soul." When life's trials assail you, why don't you allow God to take you by the hand and lead you through the trial to the "spring" of refreshing, restoration, and joy?

Lord, when I'm facing the trials of life, please remind me to take Your hand and let You walk me through them. As You restore spring, please also restore my soul and my joy.

God's Will

The world and its desires pass away, but whoever does the will of God lives forever.

—1 John 2:17

H ave you ever felt as if you were missing something? Day after day your life slips by and you're certain there must be more. The surest way to live a joyless life is to live outside of God's will. Our hearts will never be at peace and our souls will never be satisfied until we're doing what we were created to do.

It's easy to get caught up in what school to go to, what career to choose, and where to carry out our lives. Ultimately, none of the major life decisions we make will bring us joy if they're not made with God's will in mind.

But what is God's will? We are to seek justice for the oppressed (Isaiah 1:17). Christ followers, as a whole, should be known for kindness (Colossians 3:12). Humility should be evident in our lives (Numbers 12:3). We'll begin living joyfully when all of our life decisions are based upon God's will.

Teach me to seek Your will, Lord, in every decision I make. Give me the joy that comes from living according to Your Word.

Joy for Those Who Defend

But give great joy to those who came to my defense. Let them
continually say, "Great is the LORD, who delights in blessing his
servant with peace!"

—Psalm 35:27 NLT

Sometimes we're tempted to jump into a conversation in which a couple of friends or colleagues are belittling a third person. Gossip is easy. Refusing to take part in gossip, on the other hand, can be awkward. And actually coming to someone's defense can be downright challenging.

"You know, Susan's very likeable if you take a moment to get to know her."

"Sorry, guys, but that story you're telling about Bob is just a rumor, and I don't want to be a part of it."

In today's psalm, David (who spent quite some time running from his enemies) asked the Lord to "give great joy to those who came to [his] defense." David's defenders had risked their very lives for his sake. The New International Version states that they "delight[ed] in [his] vindication." In turn, David spoke blessings on them, asking the Lord to grant them joy. Today, whom can you defend?

Lord, please bless with great joy those who have come to my defense.
Help me to be the one in the crowd who defends rather than
slanders.

Flawless

As for God, his way is perfect: The LORD's word is flawless.
—Psalm 18:30

I f you've ever read stories about the gods and goddesses of ancient Rome and Greece, you know that they were anything but flawless. Most of them engaged in immoral sexual behavior, many were hot-tempered, and all were unpredictable and capricious. We, however, have a living God who is perfect, sinless, "slow to anger," loving, and unchanging (Exodus 34:6). What the Lord said two thousand years ago is absolutely true and dependable today. The Bible says He's "the same yesterday and today and forever" (Hebrews 13:8).

How joyful we can be that our God is totally dependable and sinless! When we cry out to Him for help, we can know without a shadow of a doubt that we'll receive an answer, and that answer will be absolutely loving and without error. No human counselor can make that promise! Neither can any man-made "god" or "goddess."

Vow today that you'll take every trouble, every question, every wrongdoing you're dealing with straight to the Lord and to His Word, the Bible. You *will* receive your answer!

Lord, I rejoice that whenever I take a problem to You, I can be certain that I'll receive the perfect answer. You are faithful, Lord, and Your Word is perfect!

Refuge of Joy

But let all who take refuge in you rejoice; let them ever sing for joy, and spread your protection over them, that those who love your name may exult in you.

—Psalm 5:11 ESV

There are things that scare us as adults that probably didn't faze us as children. Tornadoes are a great example. This scene has played out many times: parents hustle their children into the basement for safety, and while the adults listen to the weather radio, the children play games, trusting Mom and Dad to handle the scary stuff.

What currently scares you? It could be a situation that needs to be dealt with, a health concern, or something happening in the news. Have you ever turned to something or someone for safety and been let down? It's unnerving to realize that you're vulnerable.

The psalmist understood that the only true refuge is found in the Lord. When we trust God to watch over us and protect us, things that scared us before will not even faze us now. We can sing for joy in any circumstance. We can trust our God to handle the scary stuff.

The world can be a frightening place, Lord. I am so grateful that You are a place of refuge for Your people.

Furbaby Joy

The wolf will live peacefully beside the wobbly-kneed lamb, and
the leopard will lie down with the young goat; the calf and yearling,
newborn and slow, will rest secure with the lion; and a little child
will tend them all.

—Isaiah 11:6–7 VOICE

ore and more healthcare providers are recognizing the long-term benefits of owning a pet. Having a pet is a proven stress-reliever and can improve one's mood considerably. Petting a cat can lower blood pressure and will counteract loneliness by providing a much-needed connection with another living thing. Dogs have been known to reduce depression because of their comical antics and unreserved joy and affection.

Animals are a gift from God. They are a wonderful part of God's beloved creation. He continues to show His care for animals every day. In fact, the movie *All Dogs Go to Heaven* might be more accurate than we suspect, as animals are mentioned several times in the book of Revelation. If you're deeply connected to your pet, don't feel silly, and don't try to explain it away. Instead, shower the Lord with gratitude for this precious gift. And, if your pet is well-behaved, consider getting permission from your local nursing home to visit residents. Share the joy!

Thank You so much, Lord, for the joy I experience because of my
furbaby. Thank You for such a precious gift.

True Prosperity

Blessed is the one . . . whose delight is in the law of the LORD, and who meditates on his law day and night. . . . Whatever they do prospers.

—Psalm 1:1–3

Imagine if everything you set your hand to turned out just beautifully. Think of the satisfaction, the sense of accomplishment, and the joy that would bring to your heart!

The first three verses of Psalm 1 give us some criteria for making this happen. One of those criteria is to "delight . . . in the law of the LORD [and meditate] on his law day and night." Mind you, the "law of the LORD" does *not* consist of the man-made laws invented by some denominations, but the pure, unchanged, and unchanging Word of God. In order to "delight" and to "meditate" on the law of God, we must first study it, and this means reading the Word *carefully, prayerfully,* and *studiously* every day ("day and night").

Many people who've made it a lifelong habit to read the Bible daily insist that, as many times as they've read the same verses, they learn something new every day. God's Word is as fresh and new and instructive today as it was two thousand years ago.

Thank You, Lord, for Your Word, the Bible. Teach me to delight in Your law.

More than Repurposed

In a flash, in the twinkling of an eye. . . . we will be changed.
—1 Corinthians 15:52

ew things are as striking as a lovingly crafted piece of repurposed furniture—for example, a dinner table made of wooden pallets or a kitchen island built from an old dresser. More and more, people are gravitating toward these sorts of pieces to adorn their homes not just because they're resourceful but because the finished pieces are lovely to look at. To have the skill to bring new life and meaning to something that appeared old, rickety, or even worthless—something that the next person would have taken to the dump—is a true gift.

God is the greatest Creator of all. The good news for us, His most precious creations, is that when we're "old and rickety," He doesn't just repurpose us, He completely transforms us. He re-created us at the moment we were born again into the kingdom, and when our earthly lives are through, He'll give us not just a refurbishment, but perfect, new bodies. What a day of jubilation that will be!

Lord, thank You for never discarding Your children; instead, You make us better and better.

Joyful Purpose

For we are God's handiwork, created in Christ Jesus to do good works, which God prepared in advance for us to do.

—Ephesians 2:10

Have you ever known someone who struggled with discovering his purpose in life? It could be a young person choosing a career or a college. It might be an older person trying to figure out what to do after retirement. It doesn't matter who they are or at what stage of life they are in, people want to know why they are alive and what they're meant to do.

Every person was created by God with a purpose. No one ever draws a single breath without good works being planned in advance for her to do. People who live knowing they have a purpose are joyful people.

God doesn't always give us the details of His plan for our lives, but we can live knowing that there is one. And it's good! As we wait for His timing, we simply do the next thing.

Long before our hearts were beating, we existed in the heart of God. There is a part of His grand plan that only you can play. He has a unique plan for every other person as well. Each plan has a purpose—and a plan with purpose brings us great joy.

It's so exciting, Lord, to be a part of Your plan. It brings me such joy knowing that I have a part to play and good works to do.

Hope of the Righteous

The hope of the righteous brings joy.

—Proverbs 10:28 ESV

Have you ever hoped for something and ended up disappointed? Maybe the thing you hoped for didn't work out. Perhaps you received exactly what you hoped for but it wasn't at all what you expected. Imagine being invited to a close friend's house for tacos. It's one of your favorite meals as a beef-lover, so you show up excited. What your friend failed to tell you was that he planned to make chicken tacos and not beef. Your tacos would probably taste a whole lot like disappointment that night.

The hope of the righteous, on the other hand, always brings joy. That's because the hope we have in Christ "will not lead to disappointment" (Romans 5:5 NLT). When we place our hope in Christ, we can have joy because we receive exactly what we hope for: forgiveness, peace, purpose, love, and so much more. Let's place our hope in the only One who can fill our hearts with joy.

To place my hope in the things of this world will always lead to disappointment. Thank You, Lord, for a hope that brings joy.

Rest

Then God blessed the seventh day and made it holy, because on it he rested from all the work of creating that he had done.

—Genesis 2:3

Are you a little grumpy when you're tired? A lot grumpy? It's okay; we're all friends here. The fact is that exhaustion doesn't bring out the joy in people. Things that wouldn't even faze us on a good day can bring out the crazy in us when we've been too tired for too long.

Everything God does has a purpose. When we read about something He did or said, we should really take note. During creation, for instance, He made a point of resting. Why would He do that? God wasn't weary from all the work (Isaiah 40:28). He wasn't about to take a nap (Psalm 121:4). God rested so that His people would follow His example (Exodus 16:30).

It's okay to take a break and be refreshed. If you find yourself missing the joy and wondering when you became so irritable, carve out some time to rest. It was important enough for God to set the example; let's follow it. Joyful people know how to rest.

I don't like the person I become when I overextend myself, Lord. Remind me of the importance of rest.

Pain with Purpose

I want you to know, brothers and sisters, that what has happened to me has actually served to advance the gospel.

—Philippians 1:12

How do you feel when you look back on painful experiences? Some things you're probably just thankful to have survived. Then there are those experiences where you're able to see the bigger picture and discern some purpose behind the pain. Maybe a tragedy brought some healing to broken relationships or caused someone to seek God. It changes everything when you can see that your suffering wasn't in vain.

Paul's letter to the Philippians is often called the "joy letter" because of its emphasis on rejoicing even in trials. How was Paul able to issue this call to rejoice after all he had endured? It was because he saw the greater purpose. Paul knew that everything that happened to him caused the gospel to be spread, and that brought him great joy.

You, too, can rejoice in the midst of pain knowing that your God can use it for His glory. Nothing you endure is ever in vain if you allow it to make His name known.

Lord, help me see the purpose behind my pain and experience the joy of allowing that pain to advance the gospel.

Use Your Gifts

In his grace, God has given us different gifts for doing certain things well.

—Romans 12:6 NLT

What activity brings you the most joy and makes you feel the most fulfilled? Chances are that your spiritual gifts are somehow connected to that activity. We'll never feel true joy until we're doing what God intended us to do.

It's tempting to begin comparing our talents with those of other people and considering someone else's gifts more valuable. There are no better or worse gifts; none of us got stuck with the leftover one. We all have differing gifts, and there's every expectation that we use them.

It's essential that we develop those gifts in order to live joyfully. Your gifting is connected to your purpose, and you'll discover true joy in living out your purpose. How are you going to use your gifts today?

Give me the wisdom to understand my gifts and the boldness to use them for Your glory, Lord.

What Do You Want to Do?

The LORD says, "I will guide you along the best pathway for your life. I will advise you and watch over you."

— Psalm 32:8 NLT

When we first fall in love, we're quick to ask our sweetheart what he or she would like to do. "You want to go see a movie? Or maybe order a pizza? Take a bike ride around town?" It doesn't matter what our loved one prefers, as long as he or she is happy.

Many Christians are familiar with this scenario, yet they've never considered asking God what He'd like to do on a given day. We forget that it's not just okay but desirable to find out the Lord's preferences regarding a workday *or* a weekend. After all, who else would know best? If we can get into the habit of asking the Lord what He wants to do with the next hour or day or week, we'll discover it sometimes differs from what we'd planned. As flawed human beings, we often prioritize our schedules according to what's hounding us most, rather than what's most important to Him.

Do you want to have a joyful week? Ask the Lord what *He* wants you to do with your time.

Lord, what do You want to do this week? What about today? How about right now?

Christ Is Proclaimed

What then? Only that in every way, whether in pretense or in truth, Christ is proclaimed, and in that I rejoice. Yes, and I will rejoice.

—Philippians 1:18 ESV

ow easily are you distracted? The fact is that there are *many* distractions in our world. There are even faith-related things that can cause us to lose focus. It's easy to get caught up in someone else's methods or motives and forget the ultimate goal.

Imagine Paul sitting in his prison cell knowing that people were preaching Christ out of envy and rivalry (Philippians 1:17). One would think that would make a guy a little bitter, right? Paul was able to see the bigger picture. He understood that Christ was still being preached and, in that, he was able to rejoice.

The purpose of any trial is to proclaim the name of Christ. We, like Paul, can rejoice in any trial as long as it's serving to advance the gospel. Do you want to live joyfully? Ask yourself, "How can Christ be proclaimed in this situation?" Then let the rejoicing begin.

No matter what comes my way, Lord, I will rejoice in knowing that Your name will be proclaimed through it all.

Unafraid

For God has not given us a spirit of fear and timidity, but of power, love, and self-discipline.

—2 Timothy 1:7 NLT

What scares you? Most people could come up with a few fears pretty quickly. Are you afraid of skyscrapers, small spaces, or spiders? Perhaps you fear being alone, being insignificant, or never quite finding your purpose in life. Whatever it is that causes fear to enter your spirit, there is one trait that is common to them all: if it causes you fear, it isn't from God.

Perhaps that's why the psalmist declared that he would not fear (Psalm 118:6) and why every gospel includes a command from Jesus to not fear (Matthew 10:26; Mark 6:50; Luke 12:4; John 14:27). Peter, when writing to those in exile, encouraged them to not be afraid (1 Peter 3:14).

For many of us, it's a constant battle. Each day, we must make a choice; we must choose joy over fear. Living unafraid is a huge step to living joyfully.

Thank You, Father, that I don't have to live in fear. Because of Your love, I can choose to live unafraid all of my days.

God's Eraser

*The LORD gave and the LORD has taken away; may the name of the
LORD be praised.*

—Job 1:21

Artists who work with pencil, charcoal, or graphite know
that a great portrait depends on not just laying charcoal
or graphite on the paper, but skillfully *removing* it. An eraser
can be just as valuable a tool as a pencil. For example, when
creating white lines (such as the whiskers in an old man's
beard), the artist first applies the medium to the paper, and
then skillfully erases it, leaving clean white streaks against a
darker background. The beauty of many works of art comes
not only from what's added, but from what's erased.

God is pleased to add blessings to our lives, but He'll
just as willingly "erase" certain things. A beautiful life is one
that involves not only the gifts God gives, but the things He
takes away because they're not good for us, or because losing them will strengthen our character and make us more
like Him.

*Lord, You're the most skilled and loving Artist of all. Please add to
my life, but apply Your eraser, too, as You see fit.*

Count Your Blessings

Every good and perfect gift is from above, coming down from the Father of the heavenly lights, who does not change like shifting shadows.

—James 1:17

Do you ever begin to feel sorry for yourself? We've all been guilty of throwing a pity party or two in our day. What we often discover is that, when it happens, it's because we've begun overlooking or taking for granted the blessings of the Lord.

It doesn't matter if it's a leather-bound journal or a piece of scratch paper, there's a lot to be said for literally counting your blessings by recording them. If you've never done this exercise or if it's been a while, you might struggle at first. But you'll be amazed at how God will open your eyes once you've made gratitude a habit.

You'll begin to find joy in freshly washed linens, the smell of a new candle, or a piece of pumpkin pie. (Anything pumpkin should always make the blessings list!) When Satan tries to steal your joy—and he will try—you can go to your journal or notebook and remind yourself of how much you have been given.

Forgive me, Lord, for the times I have taken Your gifts for granted. You are the Giver of good and perfect things, and that brings me great joy.

Wisdom Is Bliss

Happy is a man who finds wisdom and who acquires understanding.

—Proverbs 3:13 HCSB

You're probably familiar with the saying "Ignorance is bliss." It's tempting to live that way, isn't it? While it's sometimes better to be in the dark and not have to deal with the drama of a situation, Scripture says that it is actually wisdom and understanding that bring happiness.

Happiness comes when we gain the wisdom needed to make our way in this world. The Bible contains all the wisdom we need to handle any situation we may encounter or to navigate the most complicated of relationships.

Happiness also comes when we understand who we are in Christ. We were created *by* God and *in His image*. We have good works to do and have been given the gifts necessary to do them. We are so loved that Christ laid down His life for us.

Many people wander because they are lost; they don't understand who they are or why they're here, and their lack of understanding is far from blissful. We don't have to live that way. Let's be seekers of wisdom and people of understanding; this is the way to happiness.

Thank You for the wisdom and understanding found in Your Word, God. I am happiest when I know who I am in You.

Joyful Fruit

Since we have these promises, dear friends, let us purify ourselves
. . . perfecting holiness out of reverence for God.

—2 Corinthians 7:1

We've probably all heard the saying, "God cares more about our holiness than our happiness." It's certainly true that our holiness is *quite* important to God, but He doesn't necessarily choose it over happiness. It doesn't have to be an either/or scenario.

God isn't opposed to our happiness. He simply offers us something better. Holiness is always the goal, so let's remove that from this particular equation. What we need to recognize is that God longs to give us joy instead of the happiness for which we often settle.

Happiness is appealing. "Don't worry; be happy." That was the mantra of the late '80s, right? (That song is stuck in your head now, isn't it?) The problem with this adage is that happiness only lasts until the money runs out, the possessions rust out, or the romance burns out. Happiness is a fickle friend. Maybe that's why it isn't a fruit of the Spirit.

When we make the decision to follow Christ as Lord, He fills our hearts with His complete and perfect joy. Let's stop chasing happiness and embrace the joy we've already been given.

The joy You offer, Lord, is far superior to any happiness I may try to find for myself.

Shaking Off the Fear of Man

Fear of man will prove to be a snare.

—Proverbs 29:25

Satan would have us believe that our happiness hinges on how admired we are by others, but only God's approval will bring you the joy that fulfills.

The next time you catch yourself fretting about others are thinking about you, ask yourself: *What do they have that I need so badly?* Then ask yourself whether you need to be trying to meet that need through them—or through God.

Here's a nugget that might hurt your pride even as it frees you from the fear of people: usually, people aren't watching you with the intensity you imagine. Satan wants to convince us that everyone is honed in on our every move, but usually they're preoccupied by other things. While you're agonizing during the worship service because you'd love to raise your hands but you're worried about what people might think, it's unlikely that anyone but the bored little boy to your left is, in fact, watching you.

The energy we spend fretting about what people are thinking would be far better spent on cultivating joy!

Lord, help me to "get over myself" and focus on You instead. Free me from the fear of people until I fear no one except You.

Secret to Joy

"I have told you these things so that you will be filled with my joy. Yes, your joy will overflow!"

—John 15:11 NLT

What if someone discovered the secret to living joyfully? Would you want them to share it with you? That's a silly question. It's safe to say we would all want in on such a secret! Bring on the joy, right?

One of the beautiful things about Jesus is that He doesn't keep secrets from us. There *is* a way to live joyfully, and He is more than willing to share it with us. "If you keep My commands," Jesus says, "you will remain in My love" (John 15:10 HCSB). He goes on to explain that He is telling the people this so that they may be filled with His joy. The secret to joy is obedience.

We can obey the Lord's commands regardless of our financial situation, social standing, or marital status. We can live joyfully even in the midst of disappointments, bad news, and rainy days. Let's live obedient, joy-filled lives.

Give me the wisdom and discipline, Lord, to live in such a way as to be filled with Your joy.

Choose Joy

Rejoice in the Lord always. I will say it again: Rejoice!

—Philippians 4:4

e wake up and remember it's Saturday, and we feel joy. We realize we left the car windows down during a rainstorm and the seat is soaked, and we fume.

We assume that joy is a product of our circumstances, but that's not true. We can *choose* joy. Paul (who endured countless circumstances that would've challenged the most resilient saint) said, "Rejoice in the Lord." And then he repeated himself for good measure: "I will say it again: Rejoice!" He wouldn't have given his readers this instruction if it weren't possible to choose joy during hardship. If we sit around waiting for joy to fall into our laps, it'll never happen. But we can learn to reach out and grab it, knowing it's ours for the taking because we're children of God.

Embracing joy means we must drop other things, like fear, bitterness, and self-pity. It's impossible to indulge in both at the same time; therefore, we can only walk in joy at the expense of the things that weigh us down. What a great trade-off!

Lord, I choose joy! I reach out and grab it right now, even as I relinquish the emotions that weigh me down.

Filled with Joy

As I remember your tears, I long to see you, that I may be filled with joy.

—2 Timothy 1:4 ESV

Who's your favorite person to be around? Is it a spouse, a close friend, or a relative? Close your eyes and imagine that person. What is it that makes you want to be in his or her presence? Whoever they may be, these people are usually our favorites because they refresh our spirits and fill us with joy.

We see in 2 Timothy that Timothy was Paul's person. Paul was enduring terrible trials and heartbreaking betrayals and he longed to see his son in the faith, Timothy. Why was he desperate to see him? Being with Timothy filled Paul with joy (2 Timothy 1:4). In this same letter, Paul also mentioned Onesiphorus as another individual who "often refreshed" him (2 Timothy 1:16). People who encourage us, point us to the Father, and fill us with joy are some of God's greatest blessings.

Let's thank the Lord for those who fill us with joy, or ask Him to bring someone like that into our lives.

We were created for joyful fellowship, Lord. Help me be a source of joy for those around me.

Joy in Certainty

So trust in the Eternal One forever, for He is like a great Rock—
strong, stable, trustworthy, and lasting.

—Isaiah 26:4 VOICE

Some people thrive on adventure. Think of the young man who packs a duffel and spends a year traveling the world with no map and few plans—what an undertaking! Whether you're venturesome or not, all humans need to know that certain things in life will never change. Even most thrill-seekers will admit to having a few people or places that give them a feeling of certainty and help them feel grounded.

But sometimes life takes an unexpected turn and suddenly the things that grounded us are gone. A loved one dies, a house is foreclosed, a job falls through. Maybe this is why God so often refers to Himself as our Rock. Again and again in the Bible, He's described as such. The word *rock* speaks of certainty, permanence, and immovability. Picture a boulder that refuses to budge an inch in spite of wind, storm, or even tornado or flood. That's our God. Living joyfully means knowing that He's as immovable as the largest boulder on the planet times a million, and then a million more.

You are my certainty, Lord! You're my Rock. You ground me when nothing else can, and I rejoice in You.

Joy in Variety

There are varieties of gifts, but the same Spirit . . . varieties of
service, but the same Lord . . . varieties of activities, but it is the
same God who empowers them all.

—1 Corinthians 12:4–6 ESV

People have a deep-seated need for certainty, but we also need change and variety. *That's contradictory*, you might say, and you're right: these two needs can work against each other. This is the reason we often struggle to make choices: we want things to remain the same, but we're ready for a change!

People aren't cut out for endless monotony. We might joke that our cat has it made—nothing to do all day except eat and sleep—but few of us would thrive that way. But unless we welcome healthy changes into our lives, we'll be tempted to break the monotony with unhealthy substitutes: a toxic relationship, too much TV, or other distractions. If you've been lacking joy because there's too much "same-ness" in your life, make one small change this week. It doesn't have to be grand or cost much (if any) money. Buy a few skeins of yarn and look up "How to crochet." Join that Bible study your friend keeps inviting you to. Spark a change, and reignite joy.

Sometimes I get bored with the same old same old, Lord. Help me
to make changes that are pleasing to You.

The Joy of Letting God Lead

Whether you turn to the right or to the left, your ears will hear a voice behind you, saying, "This is the way; walk in it."

—Isaiah 30:21

Some people have a terrible sense of direction. They'll tell you they feel as if their internal GPS is broken. They can lose their way while driving to the store even though they've been there a dozen times. Other people could be dropped into the woods at midnight with no compass and find their way out by daybreak. The "directionally challenged" are in awe of those who always seem to know exactly where they are and how to get to where they're headed. But when it comes to life, we're all in the same boat: none of us can find our way on our own. We *must* keep our eyes on Jesus at all times if we're going to navigate life as intended.

Surrendering to God's lead is liberating: the moment we do so, we're able to give ourselves to the joyful journey that is life. We can trust Him to guide us completely. Proverbs tells us, "Give Him the credit for everything you accomplish, and He will smooth out and straighten the road that lies ahead" (3:6 VOICE). What a wonderful promise!

Lord, I acknowledge that I can't find my way through life without You for even a moment. I surrender my need to lead and give myself to the joyful journey.

A Letter of Encouragement

And when they read it, they rejoiced because of its encouragement.
—Acts 15:31 ESV

In today's verse, the believers in Antioch were encouraged by a letter from the elders of the church. In recent years, we've discovered that emails, texts, and instant messages are convenient time-savers, but in the process we've lost the art of letter-writing. The tragedy is that handwritten letters, crafted with patience, care, and thought, have become rare.

The next time you're about to send a quick email to thank someone for a gift, grab a pen and paper instead. Give some thought as to how to express your gratitude. In what way, exactly, did their gift bring you joy? What was your first thought when you saw it?

Similarly, the next time you hear that a friend is struggling, resist the urge to text a praying hands emoticon and jot a note instead. Reassure them in whatever way you can: *I know today is the anniversary of your father's passing. He'd be so proud of the man you've become!*

Let's follow the elders' example and take a moment to spread a little joy through the written word.

Lord, thank You for the gift of the written word. Help me to spend the time and effort to write to someone this week.

The Joy of Wholeheartedness

All Judah rejoiced about the oath because they had sworn it wholeheartedly. They sought God eagerly, and he was found by them.

—2 Chronicles 15:15

We've all heard the adage *Go big or go home.* In today's verse, that seems to be the attitude of the people of Judah. They had just rededicated their whole lives to God. They'd torn down the pagan altars, offered a sacrifice of 7,700 animals, and sworn to seek God fervently. And then they rejoiced.

As a rule, a Christian who lives halfheartedly is not a very joyful Christian, while those who do things wholeheartedly, refusing to hold anything back from God for themselves, experience joy. Notice that when the Israelites sought God "eagerly," with holy hunger, He allowed Himself to be "found by them." What greater reward, what better motivation for putting our all into serving Jesus, than the knowledge that He'll make sure we find Him?

The next time someone tries to rein in your enthusiasm for the Lord, determine to seek Him that much more!

Like the Israelites, Lord, I rejoice about my relationship with You. Help me to live wholeheartedly and to seek You eagerly.

MARCH

Joy in the Fire

You, God, tested us. . . . We went through fire and water, but you brought us to a place of abundance.

Forest fires are devastating, but they're also necessary. Forests contain decomposed, nutrient-rich plant matter that periodically needs to be burned and reintroduced into the soil as ash so the forest stays healthy.

Many believers will tell you that the "fires" of life purified them so beautifully that they looked back at those experiences not with bitterness, but with gratitude. One reason is that when we allow God to carry us through times of grief and pain, we find out afterward that we have a greater capacity for joy and gratitude. God uses the difficult times to shape and mold us, and to pry us free from our hang-ups so we're changed for the better. When we shut out suffering and pain by trying to ignore it, or push sorrow under the surface and refuse to feel it, we unintentionally shut out joy.

We'll probably never look forward to suffering, but we *can* know we'll come out better on the other side if we just hold on tightly to the Lord and allow His fire to do its work.

Lord, thank You for making room in my heart for joy while I'm in Your fire.

No Time for Comparison

I praise you because I am fearfully and wonderfully made; your works are wonderful.

—Psalm 139:14

y kids aren't as well behaved as hers." *So*? Good behavior is nice, but it's no guarantee that a child will grow up to be a world-changer for the kingdom.

"He earns more money than I do." *And*? A fat checking account can purchase some creature comforts, but what does it have to do with the things that really matter?

"She's so much prettier than I am." *So*? Think about the people you admire most: Mother Teresa. Abraham Lincoln. Jesus Christ—you know, the One who "didn't look like anything or anyone of consequence—he had no physical beauty to attract our attention" (Isaiah 53:2 VOICE).

"Comparison is the death of joy," said Mark Twain. You're nothing like anyone else because you're not supposed to be. The world needs your unique personality, your particular talents, sense of humor, and perspective. Don't dishonor God by implying that He missed the mark when He made You. Stop the comparison game, and rejoice in who you are: a one-of-a-kind child of God.

Lord, forgive me for comparing myself to Your other sons and daughters. I will rejoice in my distinctiveness.

Righteousness and Justice

And the heavens proclaim his righteousness, for he is a God of justice.

—Psalm 50:6

The elderly man stood, dazed and confused, at the exit gate to the state penitentiary, shaking his head in disbelief. After thirty-five years in this den of horrors, he was being released. The primary witness in the prosecution's case against him had come forward; knowing she was dying, she couldn't bear the guilt of what she'd done any longer. She finally admitted she'd wrongfully accused the man, who had been convicted purely on her "positive" identification of him as the person who'd killed her husband.

Justice is a virtue that's always been rare in our world. We're staggered when we read stories like the one above, or when we hear about respected judges accepting bribes. If we're believers in the Lord, however, we can be absolutely assured that there is, indeed, justice, and His name is God Almighty. Even the heavens proclaim that He's righteous and a God of justice. We can rest in the hope and the joy of knowing justice *will* prevail.

I praise You, Lord, because You're a God of justice. I'm so happy there's hope for those who have been wrongly punished. Thank You for vindicating them!

No Such Thing as Worthless

Even before I was born, God chose me and called me by his marvelous grace.

—Galatians 1:15 NLT

The series *Antiques Roadshow* has been popular since 1979—more than thirty-five years! We love to watch breathlessly while the appraiser assesses item after item, because we never know when he might tell someone that his dusty knickknack is worth six thousand dollars. Have you wondered if you've ever inadvertently thrown a rare and priceless treasure in the garbage?

Maybe you feel as if you've been discarded by those around you. Or perhaps you feel "less than" your peers—less talented, less intelligent, less attractive, less valuable. If so, take joy in the knowledge that you've already been assessed and found to be priceless. Your own Creator has considered and evaluated you through the filter of His Son's blood, and He's declared you absolutely perfect! And who are you to argue with the all-knowing One? Rejoice! He says there's no such thing as a worthless human being. When He declares you priceless, He's not doing so because He wants you to like Him, He's declaring truth.

Even when I feel worthless, Lord, my spirit knows better: I'm priceless to You, and that's what matters most.

The Joy of a Disciplined Thought Life

We demolish arguments and every pretension that sets itself up against the knowledge of God, and we take captive every thought to make it obedient to Christ.

—2 Corinthians 10:5

any people believe they have little control over their thoughts. "I worry *all* the time about my teenagers; I'm constantly stressed out!" they complain, as though they have no choice in the matter when their thoughts run amok. But we're instructed to make any thought that contradicts truth "obedient to Christ." The language might suggest that taking control of one's thought life is exhausting work, but it's actually pretty simple and straightforward: to "demolish" and "take captive" a fearful, impure, or stressful thought, suffocate it—that is, turn your attention away immediately, giving it no time to develop—not even a split second! Instead bring your attention back to the present, back to the truth—for example, that He cares for your teenagers and will not desert them.

You *can* give your attention to thoughts that are beneficial, pure, and joyful.

Lord, teach me how to take my thoughts captive and turn my attention to the things that bring You joy.

Think About Such Things

Whatever is true, whatever is noble, whatever is right, whatever is pure, whatever is lovely, whatever is admirable—if anything is excellent or praiseworthy—think about such things.

—Philippians 4:8

The human brain is beautiful and complex, sending signals at a rate as high as 268 miles per hour. Each day, the average person entertains roughly seventy thousand thoughts. That's more than forty-eight unique thoughts every minute!

No wonder our thought lives are so crucial regarding who we are, what we do, and how we feel. Doesn't it make sense that if we fill our minds with negative, sinful, or empty thoughts, we'll accomplish little of value and struggle with fear, sin, depression, or all the above? Conversely, when we think about what's pure and noble, such as how to love our spouse well, serve our community, or raise children of character, we'll realize the dreams God puts in our hearts, and we'll have joy.

Each day holds a multitude of opportunities to concentrate on bad news, engage in gossip, surrender to pessimism, and so forth. It also holds a multitude of opportunities to focus on the things that please God. What will you fill your mind with today?

Lord, I promise that today I'll resist negative, harmful thoughts and instead focus on praiseworthy thoughts that result in joy.

Get Alone

Jesus often withdrew to lonely places and prayed.

—Luke 5:16

It's easy to become obsessed with platforms and popularity. A person might be tempted to gauge her worth by the entries on her social calendar or the number of friends in her immediate circle. While there's nothing wrong with a crowd, there's something to be said for spending time alone.

Sometimes this concept applies to a person's spiritual life as well. A person could easily fill his or her days with group Bible studies and church fellowships—and, again, there's nothing wrong with those activities. Yet there's a soul-refreshing joy that's found in stepping away from the crowd and getting alone with God.

Jesus would often withdraw to lonely places. He wasn't being ignored or pushed aside. Jesus voluntarily stepped away and chose to be alone with God.

Friends are a beautiful gift, and blessed is the man or woman who has true ones. But the best friend can't compare to the joy of being alone with the One who gave His life for us.

Being alone with You, Lord, fills my heart with unspeakable joy.
When my soul is feeling weary, I will slip away to be with You.

Responding Versus Reacting

In your anger, do not sin.

—Ephesians 4:26

arried people who are secure in themselves and in their partners usually bounce back quickly from disagreements. Often the one who feels slighted by the other will neither ignore it nor blow it out of proportion; instead, they'll voice their concern so that together they can hash things out, then move on and enjoy each other again. The Bible doesn't teach us that we can't have differences of opinion—only that we should do so without harming one another, harboring a grudge, or keeping score. It's entirely possible for two people to disagree without wounding each other and without sinning. The key is to *respond* rather than *react*. Anyone can react, but only the disciplined person can respond thoughtfully and lovingly.

Those who are easily offended are not joyful people! To be Christlike and joyful is to be unruffled in spite of a disagreement. Don't attempt to avoid every dispute, but do always handle them with grace. Remember: don't react—respond.

I rejoice in Your grace that makes it possible for me to have disagreements without hurting anyone.

The Joy of Radical Living

The promise is for you and . . . for all whom the Lord our God will call.

—Acts 2:39

We often hear the term *radical Christianity* these days, but what does this phrase mean when it comes to *your* life? Only you and God can figure that out. What constitutes radical Christian living for you might not look anything at all like it does for your best friend, spouse, or pastor. We must resist the temptation to give the term too narrow a definition, or to make quick judgments about whether someone is living a radical life for Jesus.

One person might be called to sell everything and join the mission field in some remote jungle full of eight-inch flying insects. The next person might long for a jungle adventure but be appointed to live a peaceful life and "tend the picket fence" so she can bring calm into the lives of others. Both missions are holy, and both bring deep joy to the one who obeys the call.

Anytime the Lord asks us to live out our faith in a new way, our responsibility is to joyfully answer the call—not to compare it to our neighbor's call.

Lord, I want to live a radical Christian life, no matter what that looks like. Thank You for the specific mission You've given me.

The Joy of Living Courageously

You will have success. . . . Be strong and courageous.
—1 Chronicles 22:13

ust as the definition of radical Christianity varies from person to person, so does the definition of *courage*.

What represents a courageous act for one person may not look the least bit daunting to the next, and vice versa. For example, Jane Doe enjoys public speaking, while John Doe is nauseated at the thought. When God calls John to change careers, he's thrilled, but Jane, who likes predictability, has to summon a great deal of courage to say, *Yes, Lord.*

God calls His children to leaps of faith, and in the same breath He says, "Be strong and courageous" (Joshua 1:6). The passionate Christian won't be satisfied unless he's following God in a way that requires courage; that's what we're all built for, and anything less will eventually make us restless. Each new challenge from God calls us to new heights and reminds us that the Christian life isn't for cowards. And each challenge is cause for great joy: what an honor to be called by the Lord!

Lord, I'm ready for a new challenge, and I know You'll grant me the courage to say yes.

The Joy of God's Precepts

*The precepts of the LORD are right, giving joy to the heart. The
commands of the LORD are radiant, giving light to the eyes.*

—Psalm 19:8

What must the author of Psalm 19 have been thinking
to have had such high praise for rules? How many of
us have ever thought, *Thank you, Mom and Dad, for requiring that I be
home by midnight*? or *Thank you, Boss, for ordering me to have this report
done before I can go home tonight*? Yet God was being praised for
1) the rightness of His laws, 2) giving joy to our hearts by
providing these laws, 3) His "glowing" commands, and 4)
the understanding His laws give us. Can we, in our hearts,
also thank God for all His rules and regulations?

The more you study the Word of God, the more you'll
come to see and understand that God is never capricious.
He doesn't create rules to irritate us or because He has
nothing better to do. He always *knows* what's best for us, He
always *wants* what's best for us, and He always *does* what's best
for us.

And that's reason to be joyous.

*Thank You, Lord, for Your precepts and commands because they
lead me on the straight way to You.*

The Power of Words

Anyone who is never at fault in what they say is perfect.

—James 3:2

In 2014, Ford Motor Company recalled more than a million vehicles. Most of these needed to be checked for a flaw in the power steering mechanism that had caused fifteen accidents. No doubt this recall was very expensive and time-consuming, but it had to be done. A vehicle has extreme power and can help us carry out thousands of important tasks, but that power will equal disaster if the steering mechanism isn't functioning.

Words are astoundingly powerful as well. Think about it: through the pure words of God, the entire universe came into being. Sadly, our words aren't always pure—but they're still powerful. James said our tongues could direct the whole course of our lives (James 3:6).

We're so easily drawn into wrong conversation that joyful living is possible only when our minds are set on Jesus: only then it is really safe to speak! When we're not controlled by the Lord, we're like trucks barreling down the highway minus the steering wheel. When He's in charge, we'll know the joy of pure and positive speech.

Lord, thank You for the privilege of speaking into other people's lives. Help me to do so with reverence, compassion, truth, and kindness.

The Joy of a Subdued Tongue

Peacemakers who sow in peace reap a harvest of righteousness.

—James 3:18

Search Google for *cutest animal* and you might pull up a few videos of the slow loris, with its adorable face, soft fur, and huge eyes. But do a little research and you'll discover that these animals also have a toxic bite and a sublingua— that is, a second tongue. Sadly, though we long to please God, when we chip away at others with our words we're like the slow loris, with a forked tongue and poisonous bite.

But here's the good news: if God's Word tells us, "Keep your tongue from evil and your lips from telling lies" (Psalm 34:13), then it must be possible by God's grace. Each evening, take stock of your words. Was your tongue hostile to God in any way? Are the reputations of other people safe in your hands?

You *can* know the peace and joy that come from a tongue that builds others up and never tears them down.

Lord, help me to never "let any unwholesome talk come out of [my mouth], but only what is helpful for building others up according to their needs" (Ephesians 4:29).

Focus on the Lord

Therefore my heart is glad, and my whole being rejoices; my flesh also dwells secure.

—Psalm 16:9 ESV

Have you ever observed someone and wondered, *How do they do it*? Maybe it was the way they seemed to have everything under control, how they handled a certain situation, or simply their pleasant demeanor. One of the great things about Scripture is that most of the time we don't have to wonder what it means; the message is pretty clear.

Do you want to find the Lord? It's easy; just seek Him (Proverbs 8:17). Do you desire wisdom? It's simple; just ask for it (James 1:5). Do you want a heart that is glad and a whole being that rejoices? David told you exactly what to do.

In this verse, David declared that he had joy and security. We don't have to wonder how he did it because he told us in the previous verse: "I keep the LORD in mind always" (Psalm 16:8 HCSB). By always keeping the Lord as the focus of our energy and attention, we can have glad hearts and joyful spirits.

No matter what is going on around me, Lord, keep my focus on You. Only then will my whole being rejoice.

Joy in the Unexplainable

For now we see only a reflection as in a mirror; then we shall see face to face. Now I know in part; then I shall know fully.

—1 Corinthians 13:12

aybe you've heard the question *Can the Lord make a rock so big He can't pick it up?* This might seem silly, but it illustrates the fact that we simply can't understand a being who's all-powerful and eternal. Our brains can't grasp concepts like omniscience and infinity, so when we ask certain questions, we eventually end up at an impasse. The atheist uses this impasse as an excuse to discount God: *Your God makes no sense! Your religion is foolishness!* But the child of God can actually take joy in the fact that God is unexplainable. Think about it: Do you want a God you can explain? How much faith could you put in a God who could be quantified and rationalized?

Our God is so much bigger than we are that no human being will ever completely understand Him. Even if you have lots of questions that seem unanswerable, rejoice—your God is awe-inspiring and more than anyone can grasp, and that's *great* news.

Lord, You're so big and vast and amazing, I can't comprehend You! I can't wait for the day I'll "know fully."

Restore the Joy

Restore to me the joy of your salvation and grant me a willing spirit, to sustain me.

—Psalm 51:12

Have you ever felt as if your joy tank was just about empty? What did you do to try to refill it? We may try any number of things to restore our own joy. We may plan a night out with friends or a weekend away by ourselves. Perhaps we turn to a hobby that has brought us pleasure in the past. Here's the problem: only God can restore the kind of joy our souls need.

David knew what to do when his joy was beginning to wane. He simply made his request to the One who is able to fulfill our need for joy. James may have been referring to wisdom when he said to ask "God, who gives generously" (James 1:5), but God's generosity has no limits.

If there is a need for joy in our lives, let's ask Him for it.

Fill me with Your joy, Lord. There is nothing else that cheers my heart like the joy of Your salvation.

What Really Matters

For I want you to understand what really matters, so that you may live pure and blameless lives until the day of Christ's return.

—Philippians 1:10 NLT

Have you ever looked back on a situation and realized it wasn't worth the emotional energy you put into it? Not only did you waste time worrying and fretting, you also missed out on more productive activities. Most likely, none of us can think of a single time we looked back and thought, *I'm so glad I worried about that.*

When Paul wrote his letter to the Philippians, it was important to him that they were able to discern what really mattered in life. This is also a key element in our efforts to live joyfully. When we love well and seek wisdom (Philippians 1:9), we can focus our energies on things that truly matter.

How can we know we're being distracted from what is excellent? Things that don't matter drain our joy. When we're doing the things that God deems important, we'll experience the joy of being obedient.

Lord, show me what's important to You. Those are the things I want to spend my time and effort doing.

Free to Choose

The LORD your God will . . . make you successful in everything you do.

—Deuteronomy 30:9 NLT

magine hiking a new trail with some friends and coming across a fork in the road offering two great options. One arrow points to the right: *Osprey Falls*—and another to the left: *Eagle Canyon*. You might discuss which way to go, but you certainly won't argue with your fellow hikers about which choice is right and which is wrong because both are clearly good options.

Sometimes in life, however, we forfeit our joy by agonizing over two choices because we're convinced that one is inferior to the other. Pursuing God's will is always good, and frequently one option *is* best, but have you considered that sometimes God lets us choose because He's pleased with either alternative? If you're facing a crossroads and your prayers for direction seem to be going unanswered, this might be one of those times when you're free to pick the falls *or* the canyon. God is capable of bringing His plans for you to pass, whichever you choose. Make your decision, rest in His love, and then enjoy the next adventure.

Lord, You know the decision I'm making in my life right now. I rejoice that You've given me the wisdom to choose well, and that You're always with me.

Satisfaction

You open your hand; you satisfy the desire of every living thing.
—Psalm 145:16 ESV

Have you ever craved something, but once you obtained it you were left unsatisfied? It's apparent that people have always struggled to fill the void inside. Striving to find satisfaction or love in the things of this world will always lead to emptiness and frustration.

Joy comes when we finally understand that only God can satisfy the desires of our hearts. We try to find satisfaction in countless other ways and are always left disappointed and wanting more. Solomon, with all of his wisdom, knew that nothing we see or hear while here on earth ever brings the contentment we crave (Ecclesiastes 1:8).

God holds within His hand everything we need to be joyfully satisfied. As a preacher once said, "God is good and He is generous with His goodness." It pleases Him to satisfy our desires and to see us rejoice in His goodness.

My heart will never be joyful until I learn that You, Lord, are the only source of satisfaction for my soul.

What You Don't Know

Trust in the LORD with all your heart and lean not on your own understanding.

—Proverbs 3:5

How comfortable are you admitting that you don't know something? Depending on the situation, it can be quite humbling. Yet, many times in our lives, we just don't understand.

One key to living a joyful life is to be content not knowing what you can't know. While we're certainly instructed to pursue wisdom, we don't need to become distracted attempting to understand God's playbook. Scripture advises us that His ways are far higher than our ways.

To trust the Lord with every detail of our lives frees us up to love others without restraint. Learning to not lean on our own understanding relieves a lot of pressure that we often put on ourselves to know, comprehend, and be able to explain everything.

When we learn to trust the Lord with the things we don't understand, and when we become comfortable with what we're simply not meant to know, the joy will come.

I'm okay not knowing what I can't know, Lord. I'll fully trust You and live joyfully because of that trust.

Listen

"Oh, that my people would listen to me! Oh, that Israel would follow me, walking in my paths!"

—Psalm 81:13 NLT

Have you ever gotten yourself into trouble because you weren't paying attention? It's easy enough to mess up a recipe or a relationship by not taking the time to listen. There were several instances in Scripture where not listening caused some problems. In Psalm 81, the Israelites were suffering the consequences of not listening to God.

The person who doesn't listen to God can never experience the benefits of His wisdom and guidance. We find true joy in being still and listening to what He has to say. God told the Israelites that if they would just listen to Him, they would receive provision (Psalm 81:10) and protection (Psalm 81:14).

To live joyfully, we must listen to the Word of the Lord. Listening will help us navigate difficult times. When tempted to give in to doubt or despair, choose to listen for God's voice and experience the joys that come from heeding His Word.

Lord, give me ears that are quick to listen and a heart that is quick to obey. Only then will I experience a joyful life.

Sincere Faith

*The goal of this command is love, which comes from a pure heart
and a good conscience and a sincere faith.*

—1 Timothy 1:5

Think about how you behave in the world. Would you consider your behavior exemplary? How we conduct ourselves, especially as we interact with other people, can determine whether or not we live with joy.

Two behaviors that will drain the joy from our lives are overcommitting ourselves and attempting to please everyone. For some reason we buy into the idea that busier is better. We say yes to everything and wonder when life became so complicated. In an effort to make everyone happy, we may behave in ways that do not reflect our character, morals, or values.

Paul, who wrote extensively about joy, had a clear conscience about how he conducted himself in the world. The key to a joyful life is to live simply and sincerely. Let's do what God called us to do and be the people God called us to be, and we'll begin to experience the joy of a clear conscience.

*Lord, teach me the joy that comes from living a simple and sincere
life.*

Keeping It Simple

For our boast is this . . . that we behaved in the world with simplicity and godly sincerity, not by earthly wisdom but by the grace of God.

—2 Corinthians 1:12 ESV

If you think about it, you'll realize that many (if not most) activities and events that regularly produce joy in your life are surprisingly simple. For example, devoted runners will tell you there's no joy quite like covering one mile after another while breathing the fresh air. Even the difficult uphill miles, they say, are worth that "runner's high." But they'll also tell you that at the end of the day, logging five miles while wearing a Goodwill T-shirt and secondhand shorts and using one free app is just as exhilarating as it is with the help of a quality running belt, moisture-wicking socks, and two high-tech apps to track miles, heart rate, and elevation. Either way, the joy level is exactly the same. Why? Because joy, like most things in the God-life, is far simpler than we sometimes assume.

Both joy and Christianity are lofty and uncomplicated at the same time. As one clever person worded it, "Love God. Love people. Do stuff." When it comes to joy, bells and whistles are unnecessary. So keep it simple.

Help me, Lord, when I'm tempted to complicate things. I receive the simple joys You give me daily.

Splendor

His splendor is above the earth and the heavens.

—Psalm 148:13

Stand outside on a clear night and gaze up at the endless sky, sparkling with countless stars, a lovely moon smiling down at you. Imagine how vast that sky really is, and the many planets and galaxies, all following their preset orbits for thousands of years without fail. Now imagine the size and the power and wisdom of the God who created it and set it all into motion!

Did you ever wonder why God created such a beautiful world? Certainly part of the reason is that He loves beauty and chose to surround Himself with it, but He also wanted to bless us with beauty and give us a world we could enjoy, even temporarily.

Now try to imagine how beautiful heaven must be. That is far beyond our imaginings, but we know, from God's Word, that it'll be incredibly beautiful. And, because as believers we're children of God, someday that heaven will be our permanent home. What joy we can know because we're assured of such a rich inheritance!

Lord, the world You have loaned us is beautiful. Teach us to care for it so that when we leave it, it will still be beautiful for the next generation.

Enjoying Our Children

What is mankind that you are mindful of them, human beings that you care for them?

—Psalm 8:4

Pay attention the next time you're around someone you consider to be a terrific parent: chances are very good that you'll see she doesn't just love her children, she *enjoys* them. Her love for them moves beyond duty. She has fun with them and sees them as interesting little people.

If you want to raise secure, balanced kids, let them know you revel in their existence—that you genuinely like who they are as human beings. Don't be afraid to laugh aloud at the antics of your toddler or voice your feelings of delight to your tween: "You're a hoot! What would I do without you?"

The next time your heart swells while shopping with your teenager, let her know there's no place you'd rather be than in her company. If you find yourself looking forward to spending the weekend on a fishing trip with your son, tell him you can't wait until Friday. Children know that Mom and Dad "have to" love them, but they want to know they're enjoyed as well.

Thank You so much for my kids, Lord. Help me to not just love them but to enjoy them every day.

The Joy of a Clean Slate

Those who look to him are radiant; their faces are never covered with shame.

—Psalm 34:5

In the '80s movie *Wisdom*, Emilio Estevez plays a sort of Robin Hood who, along with his girlfriend, travels from bank to bank, destroying loan records in an effort to assist farmers who are suffering in a failing economy. Everyone knows that his efforts aren't a permanent fix; he can only buy them some time because the records will eventually be restored and the loans reactivated.

When Jesus wiped out our "records," He did far more than buy us some time. He wiped our slates clean once and for all. When we "look to him," we can be free of the painful emotions caused by guilt, and the result is joy. Psalm 32:2 reads, "Blessed is the one whose sin the LORD does not count against them." The man described here experiences joy not because he's kept all the rules perfectly but because he, a blatant rule-breaker, has confessed his sin, received forgiveness, and now knows that all record of his wrongdoing is gone. Forever.

Oh, the joy of a perfectly clean slate!

Lord, I grab hold of the truth that there's no longer any record of my wrongs. Thank You for purchasing my freedom.

Time-Out

"Be still."

—Psalm 46:10

In the middle of a Saturday afternoon, your six-year-old has a meltdown. One minute he's running all over the backyard or watching cartoons with friends, and the next minute he's acting out. One minute he's laughing, and the next minute he's mad as a hornet.

What do you do? You give him a time-out: "Sit quietly for a little while, and then you can rejoin your friends," you say, setting the egg timer for five minutes. The reason you resort to a time-out is that you know he was overstimulated. He needed a break from all that noise and energy. Five minutes later, he's calm and ready to get back to the business of being a happy, spirited little boy.

Has your week been overfilled with noise, events, meetings, and deadlines? Do you feel on the verge of a meltdown? Give yourself a time-out today. Reconnect with God. Sit in your favorite chair and do nothing—absolutely nothing—for fifteen minutes. Get your joy back.

Lord, when I'm out of sorts, prompt me to stop and take a time-out with You.

Finding Joy

Glory in his holy name; let the hearts of those who seek the Lord rejoice.

—1 Chronicles 16:10

ave you ever lost something really valuable or important? Did you look in every possible place only to come up empty-handed? We all have. It's quite disheartening to realize that you're probably not going to find the thing you've been seeking for so long. You may even discover you're sad over not being able to find the thing you seek.

Scripture tells us that those who seek the Lord rejoice. The reason is that those who seek the Lord *find Him* (Proverbs 8:17). Every time! No one who truly seeks the Lord will walk away empty-handed, disappointed, or sad. There's guaranteed joy for those who desire His presence, for those who long for His love, and for those who just want *Him*. It's the easiest game of hide-and-seek you'll ever play because the Lord doesn't hide, and finding Him is pure joy.

Lord, I have wasted time seeking things that don't bring joy. Train my heart to seek only You.

Small Pleasures

Give thanks to the LORD, for he is good.

What would life be like without the small pleasures of life? The taste of pumpkin spice creamer in your coffee, the way your dog acts completely unglued when you come home because he's happy to see you, the scent of clean sheets at the end of a rough day. Then there are the seemingly trivial but very practical things: a favorite pen or chair, the drive-through car wash, a sturdy hammer. Is it silly to voice your appreciation for these things, or to feel joy when making use of them? Of course not.

We should never hesitate to express our thankfulness to God for the simple conveniences and small pleasures. It's impossible to thank Him too much or too often. And the amazing thing is that the quicker we are to thank the Giver for even the tiniest gifts, the more aware we'll become of just how many small pleasures there are in even the most routine day. There's nothing like a grateful heart to cultivate joy!

Lord, thank You so much for warm socks, hot coffee, my favorite jeans, and the million other small pleasures You've blessed me with.

Say "Thank You"

Give thanks in all circumstances; for this is God's will for you in Christ Jesus.

—1 Thessalonians 5:18

Just as we can cultivate joy by being grateful to God, we'll experience more joy when we learn to be thankful toward other people—and to *express* that gratitude. Too often we feel a twinge of thankfulness, but the thought fails to make its way from our mind to our mouth, and an opportunity to appreciate another human being (and perhaps improve his day a hundredfold) slips past us. Make a habit of saying "Thank you" quickly, and since we all like to know what we've done well, remember to identify what, exactly, you're thankful for.

Did the doctor's office staff return your call the way they said they would? Say so: "Thank you so much for getting back with me so soon!" Does your middle child do his chores without having to be threatened? "Wow, you're an amazing kid, and your room looks great. I appreciate it." Heartfelt, plainspoken thank-yous take little energy or time, and the reward for both giver and receiver is joy.

Holy Spirit, please nudge me anytime I'm about to pass up an opportunity to express my thanks to someone who's blessed me in even the smallest way.

Silver Lining

What does it matter? The important thing is that in every way,
whether from false motives or true, Christ is preached. And because
of this I rejoice.

—Philippians 1:18

If you pay attention, you'll discover that the people who consistently experience joy in their lives are those who see the good and positive in virtually every circumstance. Paul was an expert at finding the silver lining. In this verse, he explained to his readers that the upside of certain people preaching the gospel out of less-than-perfect motives (such as self-promotion) was that the good news was being spread. And for this he rejoiced.

What do you do when things don't go as planned? Do you naturally give in to self-pity and complaining, or do you adapt and make the best of it? Some people are able to acclimatize quickly, which brings joy in spite of uncomfortable circumstances. When an ice storm takes out their utility pole, they light a kerosene heater, bundle up the kids, and pile into the bed together for a slumber party. What one person calls a major inconvenience, another calls a chance for a family adventure.

Let's learn from Paul to extract every bit of good out of our troubles.

Lord, make me slow to complain and quick to find the good in every
situation.

APRIL

Joyful Satisfaction

My soul will be satisfied as with fat and rich food, and my mouth will praise you with joyful lips.

—Psalm 63:5 ESV

Think about the food that satisfies you the most. What are you envisioning? Is it your mom's lasagna, Grandma's meatloaf, or perhaps a nice, tall slice of cheesecake? (Let's take a moment to thank the Lord for allowing us to live in a world with cheesecake.) Don't you love that, when the psalmist described a satisfied soul, he didn't compare it to steamed broccoli?

What made the psalmist praise the Lord with joyful lips? He found satisfaction in the Lord. He understood that the faithful love of God was "better than life" (v. 3). Nothing could fill him, complete him, or make him whole quite like the love of the One who created him.

If you have ever ordered lasagna at a restaurant and expected it to taste like your mom's, you probably did not leave satisfied. Nothing is as good as the real thing. Likewise, once we get a taste of the love of God, nothing else will bring us satisfaction or joy.

Nothing satisfies our souls like You, Lord. You are the source of all our joy.

Rejoice with Those Who Rejoice

Rejoice with those who rejoice; mourn with those who mourn.

—Romans 12:15

Be honest: When someone you know is blessed, do you feel joy? Or is your first emotion jealousy? A joyful person is quick to rejoice not only when he or she succeeds or experiences something wonderful, but when others do too. The joyful person understands the phrase *It's not all about me*. He doesn't feel slighted when his colleague receives the salesperson of the year award. She doesn't pout when her sister gets an acceptance letter to an Ivy League college. There's no need for a Christian to act like a spoiled child who demands the biggest piece of cake because there's only so much to go around. God will never run out of blessings, and His love is infinite.

The word *rejoice* sounds like *joy* for a reason. You simply can't rejoice without feeling joy. Sometimes we forget that one of the greatest benefits of rejoicing with those who rejoice is that when we do, our joy is multiplied. Let's learn to respond with kindness and enthusiasm every time God blesses one of His children.

Lord, free me of all insecurity so I can genuinely rejoice when someone else rejoices. Thank You for being such a generous Father.

Joyful Heritage

Your statutes are my heritage forever; they are the joy of my heart.
—Psalm 119:111

What's your most prized possession? For many of us, it's something that has been passed down from a loved one who has passed away. A certain elderly woman labeled each of her belongings with the name of the person she wanted to receive it. After she passed, each family member and friend received something that she had set aside especially for him or her, and those items became treasures that brought their recipients joy.

We tend to hold close those pieces of our heritage—whether a piece of jewelry, an antique dish, or a photograph—and we derive great joy from them. For those of us who are followers of Christ, the Lord's statutes are our heritage. The Word of God is one long love letter written from God Himself to each of us personally. Once we fully grasp that, the joy is going to overflow!

Thank You, Lord, for the heritage of Scripture and for the love and joy which accompanies every word.

Joy for Fear

Fear not; do not be dismayed.

—1 Chronicles 22:13 ESV

ear is an instant joy-killer.

Think about it: you simply can't feel joy and anxiety (or any other brand of fear) at the same time. Those two emotions don't mesh. Give in to fear, and your joy will disappear like sparkling water out of a cracked pitcher. Follow the Lord's instruction when He says, "Fear not" and you'll be delightfully surprised at how much more room there is inside your heart! You might be shocked when you realize how much energy and time you've wasted on fretting—and how much of that energy and time is now freed up for Christlike emotions such as joy, compassion, and contentment. Sometimes we don't realize how much we're investing in negative emotions until they're gone.

Are you exhausted? Do you feel as if you've lost that spark lately and you don't know how to get it back? Take an honest look at how much energy and time you're spending on the wrong emotions. Then choose joy.

Lord, forgive me if the reason I'm so tired is that I've given in to fear. I resist fear and receive Your joy.

Joy with Abandon

God has brought me laughter.

—Genesis 21:6

Joy is a gift from God; therefore, we can say with certainty that human beings were created for joy—and that includes the sort of joy that's lively, contagious, and sometimes even loud. Since all humans are created by God (and therefore made to experience joy), even those who don't know Him will exchange high fives with perfect strangers at the Super Bowl, laugh with abandon with friends, and revel in a good belly laugh during a silly movie.

Sometimes people mistakenly assume that Christian joy should be a quieter, more well-mannered version of "real joy," but there's a glaring problem with this theory: it's the joy that comes from God that's truly pure, complete, and the real thing, just as the only pure and complete form of love is that which comes from God.

So what's the conclusion of the matter? Don't squelch that delicious feeling of joy in your belly. Embrace each humorous, delightful, or pleasurable moment, even when it's a bit boisterous. God is probably laughing right along with you.

Lord, I receive all the joy You have for me! Thank You that I get to share big, generous doses of it with You and Your children.

Joy in the Shadows

God, Your faithful love is so valuable that people take refuge in the shadow of Your wings.

—Psalm 36:7 HCSB

hanks in part to all the mystery books, movies, and TV shows, we have come to fear walking in the shadows. Death and destruction reportedly linger in the darkness. But the Bible tells us that the place to be is in the shadow of the Lord. Plenty of Bible verses speak of hiding in, or taking refuge in, or even dwelling in the shadow of God's wings. Like children who huddle together under the bed-covers during a storm, we find safety and security in the idea of nestling under the Lord's wings. Just the *shadow* of those wings is enough to protect us!

God didn't need to handle the planets to create them and set them in motion; He doesn't have to physically touch us to heal us; and He can protect us without actually wrapping His arms (or wings) around us. In each case, all He needs to do is to think the act, and it will be done. Likewise, all we need to do is place ourselves in His shadow to be completely secure.

It gives me great joy, Lord, to know that I can find refuge and security just by being in Your shadow. I choose to place myself there.

Forever Kind of Joy

The grass withers and the flowers fall, but the word of our God endures forever.

—Isaiah 40:8

What brings your heart joy? Is it family, the ocean, or homemade bread? (Some would argue that Gary Chapman's sixth love language should involve homemade bread, melted cheese, or chocolate ice cream.) We all know that those types of things only bring temporary joy(ish) feelings. Families all have drama, oceans contain jellyfish, and bread—well, it eventually dries out.

You'll be glad to know that there's good news. Our joy does not have to be temporary if we, like the psalmist, find it in the Word of the Lord. Isaiah declared that, while other things may wither and fade, "the word of our God endures forever." Can you imagine a joy that lasts forever?

If we would train ourselves to look to the Word for joy and fulfillment, we would never be disappointed. We can hide His Word in our hearts (Psalm 119:11), and no one can ever take that away from us. It will never run out, dry out, or walk out. It is a joy that is readily available to us at all times. Let's take advantage of it!

All too often, Lord, I have looked for joy in temporary things. Thank You for the Word that never fades away and can be a fountain of joy tucked deep within my heart.

Bite of Joy

When your words came, I ate them; they were my joy and my
heart's delight, for I bear your name, LORD God Almighty.

—Jeremiah 15:16

Think about that one dessert that you simply can't resist. Is it a caramel pie? Chocolate cake? Grandma's banana pudding? Or maybe it's bread pudding. If so, when it's on the menu, a piece of it is coming your way. And, when it shows up, you are going to eat it. You're not simply going to look at it, or smell it, or post a picture to social media. When something that fabulous is before you, you eat every single bite.

When the words of the Lord came to Jeremiah, he said, "I ate them." Don't you love that imagery? He didn't just hear them. He didn't just pass the words along. No, Jeremiah took them in and let them settle deep within, and when he did, they brought him joy. When Jeremiah filled himself with Scripture, he filled himself with joy.

If we want to be filled with joy, we need to be filled with the Word of God. Let's learn to gorge ourselves on truth.

Your words, Lord, are an absolute joy to me. Speak to me, for I will
not let a single one of them go to waste.

The Donkey

"You will find a young donkey tied there. . . . Untie it and bring it here."

—Mark 11:2 HCSB

uthor Max Lucado's books have sold more than 92 million copies. Reverend Billy Graham has preached to more than two hundred million people during a span of more than five decades. Some Christians spend their whole lives making an impact for Jesus in the lives of an immeasureable number of people. Meanwhile, you work your modest job with its modest paycheck . . . or teach your Sunday school class in your little rural church . . . or write your blog with its forty-one subscribers. And you wonder, *How can I possibly be making a difference?*

When you need the joy that comes from carrying out God's will, remember the donkey that carried Jesus into Jerusalem just before the crucifixion. This little, unassuming animal might well have spent 99 percent of its life munching on grass and pulling a cart, but then one day it carried the Messiah to His final earthly destination so He could save the world. What a difference one small act of service can make!

Lord, let me serve the world by quietly serving You in the middle of my everyday life.

A Wretch like Me

But God demonstrates his own love for us in this: While we were still sinners, Christ died for us.

—Romans 5:8

Have you ever thought that someone loved you only because they had to or because you did something for them? Do you ever worry that you're one mistake away from someone no longer loving you? It's a terrible feeling to be insecure in someone's love.

On the other hand, it's a whole different feeling to know someone loves you completely and unconditionally. This kind of love has been proven over time and in difficult seasons. The love has endured when you weren't at your best and when you had nothing to give in return.

God left no doubt as to which type of love He had for His people. When God says He loves you, He's speaking about a love that came to you when you weren't even capable of loving Him in return. To know that you're loved in such a lavish way will cause you to live joyfully in that love.

Your love for me, Lord, is more than I can comprehend. It fills the deepest parts of me with an abiding joy.

Level Ground

Rich and poor have this in common: the LORD is the Maker of them all.

—Proverbs 22:2

The most joyful people are those who refuse to separate others into categories—that is, the *haves* and *have-nots*. They refuse to set themselves either above or below the rest of the human race, or to see things in terms of "us" versus "them." They understand, often because of the difficulties they've suffered in their own lives, that the bank president or the senator is only a hair's breadth—one unhappy circumstance—away from the homeless man in the soup kitchen line.

If God's given you financial security, a lucrative career, harmonious family, or lovely house, guard against overlooking others or seeing them as less important. Everyone has a story, as they say; take an interest in those stories, and you'll find that you enjoy hearing them. Find joy in people, regardless of their status or background. Don't ever stop seeing other human beings as priceless, or you'll miss out on some rewarding relationships. As the old hymn says, "The ground is level at the foot of the cross."

If I'm prone to seeing people with an "us" and "them" mentality, please forgive me, Lord, and help me to see them correctly and enjoy them as You do.

Heading Home

For the joy set before him he endured the cross, scorning its shame,
and sat down at the right hand of the throne of God.

—Hebrews 12:2

Something about home just brings joy to a person's heart. And nothing is more thrilling than knowing you're on your way home after you've been gone for a time. Not all of us can physically return to our childhood homes. Perhaps you wouldn't even desire to do so. But, as Christ followers, we are all making our way to our heavenly home.

Jesus knows what it's like to be far from home. He also knows the joy of heading home. The author of Hebrews said that Jesus was able to endure the brutality of the cross because of the joy set before Him. What *was* the joy set before Him? It was accomplishing His purpose of offering salvation to humankind. Jesus knew that after the cross came the crown. He was heading home, the Father was waiting, and it was pure joy.

Whatever you are facing in the moment, you can have joy knowing that you are only passing through. In the blink of an eye, God will swing the gates of heaven open and say, "Welcome home."

When I am in the midst of a painful trial, Lord, remind me that it does not end here. I am heading home.

Nailed to the Cross

He canceled the record of the charges against us and took it away by nailing it to the cross.

—Colossians 2:14 NLT

ll of us have that person who remembers us "when." They know the mistakes we've made: the lies, the poor relationship choices, and the downright bad decisions. It's safe to say that none of us would want to read a record of all our wrongs.

No matter how much we wish it weren't so, we all have charges against us (Romans 3:23). The offenses are great, and the enemy wants to hold us accountable for each and every one of them. Though we're all guilty, for those in Christ, there's still reason to rejoice.

When Jesus saves a person, they don't become a better version of themselves; they become someone completely different (2 Corinthians 5:17). We can have joy knowing that He's cancelled the debt and paid the penalty, and we can walk in freedom as though we'd never sinned. That's the power of the cross.

I will walk in joy knowing that my sins have been covered by the cross and I no longer have to walk under the weight of them.

Pray with Faith

"Truly I tell you, if anyone says to this mountain, 'Go, throw yourself into the sea,' and does not doubt in their heart but believes that what they say will happen, it will be done for them."

—Mark 11:23

How do you approach the practice of prayer? Are you hopeful or hesitant? Do you think it would be nice if God heard you, or are you certain that He does? James was very clear that the doubtful person could expect to receive nothing from the Lord (James 1:6–7).

Jesus also had something to say regarding prayer. To unleash its full power, we should pray for specific things. Is there a mountain in your way? Follow Jesus' instruction and command it to move. Don't be afraid to list everything you need to take place. We need to believe that God loves us enough to hear us and answer.

We can find joy in knowing that if we're asking within God's will (1 John 5:14) we can believe that we've received the thing for which we've asked (Mark 11:24). We can delight in our prayers knowing that God delights in hearing them (Proverbs 15:8).

I will train my heart to choose prayer over panic, Lord. I rejoice knowing that Your ear is always inclined to my prayers.

In the Midnight

At midnight I rise to give you thanks for your righteous laws.
—Psalm 119:62

How do you feel about the darkness? Have you ever found yourself all alone in the middle of the night? We can usually keep things together during the daytime, but there's something about the nighttime that breaks down our defenses. The psalmist had the answer for finding joy during the darkest of times.

Whatever has you feeling down and swallowed in darkness, there's joy to be found. You still have reasons to rise and give thanks. God's Word is a light, and it shines in the darkness in a way it never could in the light (Psalm 119:105). We have only to open our eyes and look for it (Psalm 119:148).

At some point, we'll all find ourselves in a dark place that we would never have chosen. Even then, if we open God's Word, He can shine His light (Psalm 119:130) and reveal places of joy.

You give me joy in the light of Your Word, Lord. I'll rise and give thanks for it even in the darkest of nights.

Cheerful Giver

Each of you should give what you have decided in your heart to give, not reluctantly or under compulsion, for God loves a cheerful giver.

—2 Corinthians 9:7

How does it make you feel to give something to someone else? Think about Christmas gifts, giving to a good cause or even buying someone's meal at a restaurant. It's pretty amazing, isn't it?

One morning, as a young woman left the grocery store with her children, an older woman walked up to her. She said that she was on a mission of joy and she handed the young mother a dozen red roses. While it certainly made the recipient smile, the joy was equally evident on the elder woman's face as she walked away.

When we think about the cheerful giver mentioned in Scripture, it's tempting to conclude that a cheerful person tends to be a generous one. While that may be true, the flip side of that is also (and perhaps more) true. A person who gives tends to be a cheerful person.

If you find yourself needing a boost of joy in your life, try being generous with your time, gifts, or finances. Become a person who gives and you'll find yourself living a little more joyfully.

Open up my eyes, Lord, to opportunities around me to give to others. Thank You for the joy that accompanies such giving.

Joy in the Future

"People will come from east and west and north and south, and will take their places at the feast in the kingdom of God."

—Luke 13:29

One of the definitions of *joy* in the *Merriam-Webster* dictionary is "the emotion evoked . . . by the *prospect* of possessing what one desires" (*italics added*). In other words, sometimes joy is the result of looking into the future.

Granted, we should guard against dwelling too much on the future because we'll miss what's happening right now. But by the same token, it's only right and natural that the promise of heaven brings joy to a Christian. Only Christ followers can delight in knowing that while the present moment is wonderful, the future will be even better . . . and that when the present moment is difficult, it'll soon pale in comparison to the future. Because we have the assurance of everlasting life, the knowledge of what lies ahead (God's unending presence, freedom from pain and suffering, the company of loved ones who have died) enhances the peaceful times and makes the sorrowful seasons bearable—or even joyful.

Today, thank God that one day you'll possess what you desire, not just for a while but for eternity.

Thank You, Jesus, that no matter what the present season is like, I know without a doubt that my future will be one of pure, unending joy.

The Joy of Music

And they sang a new song before the throne.

—Revelation 14:3

We've all basked in the peaceful sound of a wind chime outside our bedroom window or an acoustic guitar solo. Some green thumbs insist that plants grow faster when exposed to music. Babies respond with excitement to music while still in the womb! This universal love for music isn't an accident. Music comes from the mind and heart of God. No doubt this is a key reason Satan is so intent on perverting music and using it as a tool for evil.

Think about it: we don't know too much about heaven—what it looks like, how we'll spend our days, and so on—but we do know with complete certainty that it contains music! Skim the book of Revelation and you'll be convinced beyond all doubt. When used in the right way, music is heavenly—an eternal part of the kingdom of God. Embrace it, thank God for it, and find joy in it.

Lord, thank You for the sheer joy that music gives me. What a wonderful gift it is!

Shake Off the Dust

"If anyone will not welcome you or listen to your words, leave that home or town and shake the dust off your feet."

—Matthew 10:14

One of the greatest hindrances to joy is holding on to the wrong things for too long. Whether it's a toxic friendship, a romantic interest that never worked out, or the frosted lipstick you've been wearing since 1982, there comes a point in time when you just need to let go.

When Jesus sent His followers out into the world to spread the gospel, He knew they would encounter unwelcoming towns and obstinate people. Were they instructed to continue clinging to criticism and hanging out where they weren't wanted? No. "Shake the dust off your feet," was Jesus' instruction to them.

There are things worth fighting for, so please don't misunderstand. But if we are refusing to let go or move on from things that are bad for us, we will never live with any sort of joy. If we continually look to the past, we'll miss out on the joy in the present. What is standing between us and the joy in the Lord we are promised? Let's shake the dust off together.

Lord, help me discern when I need to plant myself firmly and when I need to begin shaking some dust off my feet.

Eternal Life

"Very truly I tell you, whoever obeys my word will never see death."
—John 8:51

Chances are that at some point in your life, someone close to you passed away. It doesn't matter the age of the person or whether his or her death was anticipated or sudden; the loss itself caused you grief. When a loved one dies, joy doesn't come until we understand that, as believers, we only experience the *shadow* of death.

When Adam and Eve sinned, one of the consequences was that the tree of life was no longer available to them (Genesis 3:24). God's perfect creation was marred by the introduction of death. Thankfully, God made a way for believers to once again receive the eternal life originally designed for them—God sacrificed His Son (John 3:16).

Of the many rewards promised to the one who endures, one of the most joyous is the right to once again partake of the tree of life (Revelation 2:7). The pangs of death are temporary, but the joy that comes from being in the presence of Jesus is eternal.

Thank You, Lord, that the pain of this world pales in comparison to the glories that await me in Your presence.

Joy and Grace

And the God of all grace . . . will himself restore you and make you strong, firm and steadfast.

Some people actually resist joy because they struggle with the feeling that they don't deserve it. They've made some terrible mistakes in life and failed in some major ways. The lives of those around them were affected, and not in a good way. When the choir sings their favorite worship song, or they look into the face of a brand new grandchild, their heart floods with joy—and they think, *I don't deserve this feeling!*

Can you relate? If so, you might as well know: You're right. You don't deserve to experience something as pure and lovely as joy. No one does. Neither do we deserve the love of God, the prospect of heaven—or the warmth of a shearling blanket or the taste of a good cup of coffee, for that matter . . . *except for grace.* The work of Jesus on the cross opened the door to peace, rest, beauty—and joy. Because of Him, joy is ours for the taking. Don't turn Him down. Don't resist grace and what it's accomplished.

Lord, regardless of my past sins, I receive all You have for me, including grace and joy.

Fledgling

He reached down from on high and took hold of me; he drew me out of deep waters.

—Psalm 18:16

Bald eagles build their nests far up in trees or high on the edges of cliffs. When the baby eagles, or fledglings, are old enough to begin to fly, Mama eagle will hover below the nest, flying in circles, calling out encouragement to her little ones to give it a try. When a fledgling finally launches itself into the air, Mama continues to circle the area below. If the baby eagle, for whatever reason, stops flapping his wings, Mama is right there to catch him on her back, take him back to the nest, and start the process over again.

Whether through poor choices or outright sin, each of us will occasionally lose our bearings in life and start to plummet. When that happens, God is right there, ready to catch us, set us back on our feet, and let us try again to be the Christians we should be. He never seems to tire of catching us and restoring us to solid ground. How joyful we should be that He's always there for us, always in position to rescue us!

Lord, I'm grateful that You're a God of second chances—and third, and fourth. . . . Thank You for always being there to catch me.

Time for Joy

Rejoice always.

—1 Thessalonians 5:16

f you're waiting for everything in life to be perfect in order to begin rejoicing, then here's a rather disappointing spoiler alert: life will never be all sunshine and roses; thorns and clouds will always make an appearance. Jesus said it this way, "In this world you will have trouble" (John 16:33).

Though it may not seem so at first, this is actually good news. We don't have to wake up each day and examine our current circumstances before choosing to live joyfully. Every moment of every day is the perfect time to rejoice. Paul, the same one who taught us to be content in every circumstance (Philippians 4:12), instructs us to rejoice in every circumstance as well.

Christ died so that we could live joyfully; let's embrace it. Let's rejoice when the load seems heavy because we know we don't bear it alone. Let's rejoice when there's more month than money because we know our God provides. Let's rejoice, well, always.

Thank You, Lord, that my joy is not dependent on any person or circumstance. Now is the right time to begin living joyfully.

Remember Jesus

Always remember that Jesus Christ, a descendant of King David,
was raised from the dead. This is the Good News I preach.

—2 Timothy 2:8 NLT

How are we supposed to live joyfully when everything around us is out of control? That's really the question, isn't it? How are we supposed to have joy when the news leaves us unsettled and our personal lives are in disarray? There's only one way and it almost seems too simple. Paul said it this way: "Always remember that Jesus Christ . . . was raised from the dead."

No matter what is currently going wrong, Jesus was still raised from the dead. In the midst of broken relationships, financial concerns, health scares, and heartaches, Jesus Christ was raised from the dead. That is how we can live with joy in any and every circumstance.

This good news can bring you joy each and every day because you are promised that same power (Ephesians 1:19–20). When you find yourself in need of joy, "always remember that Jesus Christ . . . was raised from the dead."

Whatever happens, Lord, I will always remember that You rose
from the dead, and I will live with joy because of it.

Tranquil Joy

For everything that happens in life—there is a season . . . a time to be quiet, a time to speak up.

—Ecclesiastes 3:1, 7 VOICE

It's been said by more than one introvert, "I might be quiet on the outside, but I'm jumping for joy on the inside." All introverts know that strong emotions can happen internally with little outward demonstration. Sometimes joy is expressed and shared with boisterous laughter, a wide smile, or an abundance of words—but often it's not. In fact, sometimes the deepest joy is expressed very quietly, even solemnly, because it's too wonderful for words. Occasionally words just get in the way.

Sometimes the loudest person in the room is the most inwardly miserable, while the quietest person is the most content. If you're naturally introverted, don't apologize for not expressing and sharing joy the way the next person does. Let your extroverted friends spread joy in their own wonderfully exuberant way; share yours one on one, with a gentle word or heartfelt hug. There's no right or wrong to it.

Lord, help me to appreciate both extroverts and introverts. Do not let me feel like I must apologize for expressing the joy You bring to my life in my own way.

Face-to-Face

I have much to write to you, but I do not want to use paper and ink. Instead, I hope to visit you and talk with you face to face, so that our joy may be complete.

—2 John v. 12

Imagine that you have something really important to share with someone you care about. Do you immediately reach for your phone to text that person? Perhaps you pull up your social media account to send her a message. Maybe, just maybe, you actually call her. These modes of communication may work, but there's something extra joyful about being face-to-face.

When John wrote 2 John, he had much to say to the church, and yet his letter is short. Why is that? It's because he felt the joy would be greater for both parties if they could sit and chat face-to-face. That's how friends speak to one another (Exodus 33:11).

It's easy to live behind a screen these days. We can convince ourselves that we're being social because we're on social media. We may have hundreds of "friends" and still have no one to listen to our good news. Let's step away from our computers and bask in the joy of a face-to-face encounter with someone today.

Thank You for the friends You have placed in my life, Lord. Remind me to take the time to see them face-to-face.

Toxins

Jesus replied, "You are in error because you do not know the Scriptures or the power of God."

—Matthew 22:29

If you want a healthy and vibrant body, there are certain things you must do: 1) avoid all toxic substances in food, drink, or the air you breathe; 2) take in (drink) plenty of water; and 3) get plenty of rest.

Likewise, if you want a clean and joyful soul, there are also certain things you must do: 1) avoid temptation and all sin; 2) take in (by studying Scripture) much of the Word of God; and 3) rest in the Lord by giving Him jurisdiction over every part of your life.

Both our bodies and our souls need much care. If we neglect either, we'll have problems that could be very costly. A sick body can cost us in trips to the doctor, pain and sickness, time with family or on the job, and money; a sick soul can cost us our joy and eternal life in heaven.

Take good care of your body and your soul!

Dear God, please forgive me for the times I've neglected my body or my soul. Help me to remember the cost of such neglect, and then to take better care of them.

God's Bristlecones

"When your limbs grow tired, your eyes are weak, and your hair a silvery gray, I will carry you as I always have."

—Isaiah 46:4 VOICE

In 1964, graduate student named Donald Currey was studying the bristlecone pines in the White Mountains of California. To determine the age of one such tree, he obtained permission from the Forest Service and cut it down—only to discover that the bristlecone was the oldest ever recorded at roughly five thousand years old. The conservation community was livid that this priceless tree had been killed because that sort of longevity is so rare. It had endured more than five thousand winters, countless storms, wind, flood, and perhaps other disasters that predate recorded history. On the outside, it was gnarled and unremarkable, but on the inside it told a different story.

Some people are like that bristlecone: average on the outside, but full of wisdom and strength on the inside from years of storms and floods. They're treasures, with many stories to tell. Living joyfully means seeing the beauty of those who've persevered—including yourself. It means rejoicing because He knows the riches that are inside you.

Are you one of God's bristlecones?

Lord, how wonderful that in Your design, age isn't a curse, but a reason for honor and rejoicing!

Tears of Joy

You hem me in behind and before, and you lay your hand upon me. Such knowledge is too wonderful for me.

Countless people have stood at the edge of the Grand Canyon with tears rolling down their cheeks because of the sheer beauty of the place. Plenty of gruff old men have taken one look at a new grandbaby and wept. We all know what it's like to feel such an overpowering surge of joy that we shed tears of joy.

It's an odd phenomenon if you think about it: Why do both sadness and joy bring about tears? Psychologists say that swinging from joy to tears is the body's way of dialing down an emotion that's too intense to handle with an opposite response. In other words, we're created to feel joy that's so powerful we can't even process it!

When David wrote Psalm 139, he was essentially saying, "Lord, the fact that You surround me and guide me in such a way that I can almost feel Your hand on my shoulder is just too much! You're so amazing, I can't handle it." Do what David did: when you feel the joy of knowing such a great God, tell Him how you feel.

Lord, I just want to tell You: You're so amazing that sometimes I can hardly contain what I'm feeling.

The Joy of Volunteerism

"In everything, do to others what you would have them do to you."
—Matthew 7:12

Ask any consistent volunteer workers why they do what they do, and they'll tell you that they feel great joy when serving others. Don't miss out on this vital part of the Christian life. If you've never volunteered (or haven't done so in a while), commit to do so this summer. And if the idea of volunteerism makes you a little uneasy, all the better: consider this a lesson in stepping out of your comfort zone.

But where can I help? you might ask. Every town has at least a few organizations that depend on volunteers to carry out their mission. Are you passionate about the sanctity of life? Contact your local pregnancy help center. Do you like to work with adults? Call your local shelter, soup kitchen, or senior center. Do you love plants or animals? Consider the community garden or animal shelter.

"There's nothing stronger than the heart of a volunteer," said WWII hero Jimmy Doolittle. There's no heart as joyful, either.

Lord, I commit to focus on others within my community. Show me where I'm most needed.

MAY

The Uniqueness of Joy

"The ostrich flaps her wings, and the ringing joy is heard."

—Job 39:13 VOICE

Your best friend jumps three feet into the air when his favorite team scores, and you can't help but shake your head. *What's wrong with him? It's just a game.*

Minutes later, you witness your daughter pampering and conversing with her beloved Pomeranian. *I've never seen anyone so ridiculously in love with a dog,* you think. *How silly.*

Later that night someone gives you the perfect cordless drill to add to your do-it-yourself collection and you practically shed tears of joy.

The very thing that brings one person joy makes no sense to the next, and vice versa. But God didn't design us as cookie-cutter versions of one another. That's why one person delights in her pottery classes, and the next can't get enough of gourmet cooking. God gave us different preferences for a reason; how boring would the human race be if we all enjoyed the same things?

God doesn't shake His head when one of His children enjoys what He's given him or her, and neither should we.

Lord, rein me in quickly when I'm critical about the ways in which other people find joy. Thank You for making us all so unique.

No Matter What

Yet I will rejoice in the LORD, I will be joyful in God my Savior.
—Habakkuk 3:18

Some of the best words in Scripture seem insignificant on the surface. Take the word *but*, for example. It may not seem like much on its own, but when it's followed by *God*, it becomes powerful. "You intended to harm me, *but God* intended it for good" (Genesis 50:20, emphasis added). The *but God* changes everything.

Another seemingly insignificant word is *yet*. Habakkuk described a bleak scenario in Habakkuk 3:17. There was no food to be found. Nothing was growing on the trees, on the vines, or in the fields. There were no sheep in the fields or cattle in the stalls. Desolation and desperation were all around. Then that sweet little word appears in the next verse. "*Yet* I will rejoice" (emphasis added). The *yet* changes everything and reminds us that our salvation means joy in any situation.

When things look bad and we're tempted to despair, let's choose to say, "Yet I will rejoice."

I will not give in to despair, Lord. Though everything seems uncertain and out of control, yet I will rejoice in You.

Pick Your Battles

Do not be afraid and do not be dismayed at this great horde, for the battle is not yours but God's.

—2 Chronicles 20:15 ESV

Nothing will steal your joy quite like fighting a losing battle. We've all done it. We've spent time, energy, and resources on a situation only to be left feeling defeated in the end. Bewildered, we've cried out to God, "I fought as hard as I could! What happened?" A key to living joyfully is to have discernment regarding which battles are ours to fight and which ones are for God to handle.

In 2 Chronicles, the people of Judah were facing a huge battle. The armies were coming against them, and they felt helpless. Before the battle ever began, they stood before the Lord and confessed that they did not know what to do (2 Chronicles 20:12). Imagine their joy when the Lord responded, "You will not have to fight this battle" (v. 17).

Whatever battles we are facing or whatever armies are coming against us, let's ask the Lord for guidance. Let's not sacrifice our joy by trying to fight a battle that is not ours to fight.

Too often, Lord, I exhaust myself fighting a losing battle. Remind me to seek Your will before ever approaching the enemy.

Joy Is Everywhere

"Build houses and settle down; plant gardens and eat what they produce."

—Jeremiah 29:5

ave you ever found yourself wishing for some future event to occur in order for you to finally be happy? We all do it from time to time. We think graduation, marriage, or retirement will suddenly bring us the joy we desire.

The exiles in Jeremiah's day just wanted to go home. They had been taken from their homes in Jerusalem and carried into captivity in Babylon. They must have been certain that they would find joy upon their deliverance. If so, God's instructions must have puzzled them. He told them to build houses, to marry and produce children who should also produce children. "Increase in number there," God said, "do not decrease" (Jeremiah 29:6).

Building homes, getting married, and having babies are joyful activities, and God was telling them that they could have those joyful experiences even in exile. We, too, can have joy wherever God has us in the moment. If you're in a hard place right now, don't give up. There is joy to be had.

Show me the joy in the journey, Lord, even when it takes me to places I never wanted to go.

Pain and Praise

Job stood up and tore his robe in grief. Then he shaved his head and fell to the ground to worship.

—Job 1:20 NLT

If you've ever endured a time of deep grief, you know that there can be some guilt involved the first time you feel joyful again. We aren't always sure if it's appropriate to laugh or worship for fear people think we're "over it." It's important to understand the nature of joy; it can coexist with myriad other emotions.

Job had just been told that his children had all been killed and he had lost all of his material possessions. Yet, in that moment when the pain seemed overwhelming, he began to worship. There are moments when joy and grief coexist. Once we realize that, we can learn to embrace the joy without guilt.

Scripture tells us that joy will come in the morning (Psalm 30:5), but for those in the midst of grief, it's important to know that joy can also come in the *mourning*. There is a point where pain and praise collide, and joy can be found there.

Teach me to embrace the joy You give in the midst of grief, Lord. Your joy is available to me in every season.

Joyful Company

*Walk with the wise and become wise, for a companion of fools
suffers harm.*

—Proverbs 13:20

How would you describe the people you hang out with?
Are they uplifting or faultfinders? Do you leave their
presence feeling drained or refreshed? We should take a
long, hard look at the people closest to us because we will
eventually become like them.

Scripture tells us that if we walk with the wise, we will
become wise. If we spend our days with negative, unhappy
people, it won't be long until we begin feeling negative and
unhappy.

In order to live joyfully, we need to surround ourselves
with individuals who exhibit the joy of the Lord. Those are
the folks we want to spend time with and allow to speak into
our lives. Let's seek out joyful company and let's seek to be
joyful company as well.

*Surround me with joyful people, Lord, and help me to be a joyful
presence in the lives of others.*

Be Content

Keep your lives free from the love of money and be content with what you have, because God has said, "Never will I leave you; never will I forsake you."

—Hebrews 13:5

ould you consider yourself a content person? Many of us often find ourselves striving for something more, better, or just different. Satan will try to convince us that we would be happy if only we had those certain things we currently lack. The truth is that, if we finally received those things, other longed-for items and events would disrupt our contentment.

A key component of a joyful life is contentment. When we realize that what God has given to us is more than enough, we are free to enjoy the life He's given. We will begin to feel joyful when our "I wish I had" pinings become "I'm so glad I have" praises.

Let's ask God to open our eyes to the blessings He has lavished upon us. We will find that when we are content with what we have, what we have is joy.

Thank You, Lord, for all that You have given to me. Forgive me for the times I have not been content with Your provision.

Trust and Obey

Jesus said to the servants, "Fill the jars with water"; so they filled them to the brim.

—John 2:7

Have you ever desired something, petitioned the Lord for it, and received something seemingly different? Have you ever thought to yourself, *That is not what I wanted at all, Lord*? If so, we understand each other. However, truly joyful people trust God when He doesn't answer the way we expected.

The immediate need for the host of the wedding in Cana was more wine. Jesus could have, with a word, refilled the wine vats and everyone could have gone on with the party. Instead, Jesus instructed them to fill six stone jugs with water. The servants immediately obeyed and, because they did, were witnesses to a miracle.

We will experience a more joyful life when we learn to trust and obey. When we look at what we've been given and don't understand why God has chosen to do it this way, we trust and obey. When our hearts long for wine and Jesus offers us water, we trust and obey. There is joy in knowing that water turns to wine in the hands of our Savior.

A joyful life is filled with trust and obedience. I will trust Your heart and obey Your Word even when I don't understand, Lord.

Filled with Joy

I meditate on your precepts and consider your ways. . . . I will not neglect your word.

—Psalm 119:15–16

For those of us blessed enough to have grown up with easy access to God's Word, it's easy to lose a little of the wonder. If the Word of God no longer brings joy to our hearts, then we're just settling for too little.

We read a catchy verse, and perhaps we share it with a friend. We post it to social media and wait for folks to like or share it. But we don't ingest it, so to speak. We don't take it in so that it can nourish us and fill us with joy. We need to be filled with the joy of God's Word!

Solomon warned about the dangers of going out into the world hungry (Proverbs 27:7). If we go out into the world with an emptiness, we will jump at anything to fill the void within. Let's spend time taking in God's Word so that we will be too full of joy to even be tempted by the world's offerings.

Thank You for Your Word, Lord. It is the only thing that fills my heart with joy and satisfies my soul.

Words of Joy

Death and life are in the power of the tongue, and those who love it will eat its fruits.

—Proverbs 18:21 ESV

We are often our own worst enemies when it comes to living joyfully. Our tongues hold the power to build up and to tear down, and unfortunately, we don't always use them wisely. Think about it: Do you ever feel better after complaining or being critical? We can never expect to have joy if our words are always negative.

James made it clear that the tongue can be a source of good things and of bad things, but not at the same time (James 3:10). This means that we need to make a choice each day. Will we choose to speak words of life which will bring joy to us and to the people around us? Or will we choose to speak words that wound our spirits and diminish our joy? The choice is ours to make. How badly do we want joy?

Let's use our words wisely and then enjoy the fruit of them.

Lord, help me to think before I speak so that I speak words of life and not death. May the fruit of my words be joy.

The Joy of Giving

And God is able to bless you abundantly, so that in all things at all times, having all that you need, you will abound in every good work.

—2 Corinthians 9:8

Fill in the blanks:

No one can cook quite like _____.

If you need someone to balance your books perfectly, call _____.

_____ has such a way with children!

Why does everyone seem to excel in at least one specific area? In what capacity do you shine? Do your friends call on you to sing at special events? Are you recognized in your workplace for your computer skills?

In today's verse, Paul was discussing money, but we can easily apply his words to other aspects of life in which God has blessed us abundantly so that we have everything we need to "abound in every good work." The New Living Translation explains that God provides generously so you'll have "plenty left over to share with others." So in whatever area you excel, learn to share that gift, remembering that obligation gives only what's necessary, but living joyfully means freely distributing to others what God has given us.

Lord, You're so generous; help me to be just like You, sharing my talents and skills—as well as monetary abundance—with others.

Almond Joy

He asked them, "Do you have anything here to eat?"

—Luke 24:41

Coconut . . . almonds . . . chocolate.

What an appropriate name: Almond *Joy*.

Fortunately for us, we're designed by God to enjoy our food. Jesus enjoyed it so much that the Pharisees criticized Him for it (Matthew 11:9), and the Gospels occasionally mention Him having dinner in this or that place. But here's the key: He never did so to excess.

Excess takes us past the place of enjoyment as God designed it, into our flesh and the demands it makes, which then leads to regret or even sin. This applies to not just food but other things in life that we're to enjoy in moderation, such as shopping or entertainment. (Have you ever sat down to watch one episode of *Cake Wars* only to come to your senses five hours later, your brain feeling like mashed potatoes?) We overstep when we take to the extreme something that God gave us to enjoy. Learn the art of moderation and you'll find new joy in "the good stuff."

What a wonderful world You've created for us to enjoy. Help me to enjoy it with moderation and gratitude.

In Pursuit of Joy

The LORD detests the way of the wicked, but he loves those who pursue godliness.

—Proverbs 15:9 NLT

Sometimes we forget that joy isn't just a nice emotion or a feeling, it's a virtue. As one of the fruits of the Spirit, joy is something we can cultivate. In fact, a solid, mature Christian is almost always a joyful Christian.

Of course we should appreciate joy when it happens, but there's no need to stop there: we should actively pursue it. This isn't the same as pursuing pleasure (which is *not* a fruit of the Spirit!). Lots of activities that bring people pleasure are a waste of time, harmful to themselves or others, or downright sinful. But joy, as God designed it, is pure and holy. Just as God is love (1 John 4:8), He's also mercy, holiness, peace—and joy. To pursue Him is to discover joy. So don't hold back! Make up your mind right now to grow in joy. Ask the Lord to allow it to spring up in your soul and "splash" all over everyone around you.

Lord, I want all the fruits of the Spirit, and I know that's Your will for me. Help me to become a carrier of joy!

Delighted

He rescued me because he delighted in me.

—Psalm 18:19

nfortunately, there are many people who can't grasp how great God's love is for them *personally.* Because we're His creations, He cherishes us—each of us. In various parts of the Bible He calls us "the apple of His eye," or His "beloved," or "the one He loves." In Psalm 18:19, He tells us He "delight[s]" in us!

Think of how you delight in a baby's smile, or how you delighted in your engagement ring, or how a forest after the rain delights your senses. Then imagine how God must have clapped His hands and laughed when you took your first breath. He was delighted! And now He still delights in you, "warts and all." It doesn't matter what you did yesterday or ten years ago; if you've repented of those sins, He delights in you.

You can also delight in the Lord. Having the God of the universe love you personally, deeply, and unconditionally should, in itself, overwhelm you with joy.

Your love, O Lord, is overwhelming. Thank You for delighting in me. I delight in You also my God, my Savior, and my Friend.

Prayer

Pray without ceasing.

—1 Thessalonians 5:17 ESV

f we aren't careful, prayer becomes an item on our to-do list that falls somewhere between loading the dishwasher and paying the electric bill. We know we should do it and we really *want* to do it. Yet, in the hustle and bustle of life, we do it, check it off our list, and move on with our day. We will never reap the full benefit of prayer treating it that way. Prayer is meant to be more than an action; it's supposed to be an ongoing attitude.

When we live with a prayerful attitude, we are constantly in contact with the One who loves us more than any other. Neglecting prayer is a surefire way to lose our joy. Prayer is our way to continually remain in the Lord's presence, and in His presence is fullness of joy (Psalm 16:11).

We can live joyfully when we pray without ceasing.

To know that You are as close as a prayer is pure joy to my heart, Lord. There is no better place than in Your presence.

Quit Comparing

Each one should test their own actions. Then they can take pride in
themselves alone, without comparing themselves to someone else.
—Galatians 6:4

Comparing your competency or success to that of another person is a fruitless endeavor. You *should* be comparing your accomplishments to your goals or your expectations, or better yet, to God's expectations. Comparing your acquisitions or worldly goods to those of others at work or in your church, family, or neighborhood is not what God wants. Someone is always left feeling like a failure.

Theodore Roosevelt is quoted as saying, "Comparison is the thief of joy." We will never be joyful people as long as we compare ourselves to someone else. We are only seeing the cropped and filtered version that they want us to see. We can have joy when we examine our own hearts and actions and compare them to the only thing that matters: God's Word.

We can have joy when we each stay in our lane and run our own race.

I will no longer allow comparison to steal my joy and distract me
from You, Lord.

Look to Him

Those who look to Him are radiant with joy.

—Psalm 34:5 HCSB

You're probably familiar with the song that has the line, "Be careful, little eyes, what you see." What we allow our eyes to see really does affect us. Our children should be taught from a very young age that protecting their eyes protects their hearts.

If we allow our eyes to view inappropriate things, we will be filled with shame. If our eyes are focused on other people's things, we can become envious. If we continually gaze upon ourselves and our accomplishments, pride may fill our hearts. It matters where we look.

Instead of focusing on where our eyes are looking, let's focus on what we want as an end result. We want to live joyfully, don't we? Then we need to stop wasting our time looking at worthless things (Psalm 119:37).

Is there a relationship that needs mending? Look to Him. Is there a hurt that needs healing? Look to Him. Are there some ashes that need to be made beautiful (Isaiah 61:3)? You guessed it; look to Him and be radiant with joy.

I have spent too much time focused on the wrong things, Lord. Let the things of this world fade until You are all I see.

Small Miracles

Ears to hear and eyes to see—both are gifts from the LORD.
—Proverbs 20:12 NLT

You're pulling into the grocery store on a busy Saturday when someone pulls out of a front-row parking spot just in time for you to pull in. Do you see this as a stroke of luck or a smile from God?

The morning after the alternator goes out on your car, your boss asks you if you want some overtime. Coincidence or small miracle?

A flock of bright red cardinals lands in your backyard the moment you look out the window. Happy accident or gift from God?

Our ability to see the small miracles and "winks from God" that happen every day—along with our willingness to thank God for them—has a lot to do with how much joy we experience. Do you need more joy? Learn to recognize the fingerprints of God all around you, and don't waste a minute before thanking Him when you encounter a small miracle in the middle of a routine day.

Jesus, give me eyes to see the small miracles that happen every day.
Thank You so much for the countless gifts You give!

Just Wait

On one occasion, while he was eating with them, he gave them this command: "Do not leave Jerusalem, but wait for the gift my Father promised, which you have heard me speak about."

—Acts 1:4

How well do you wait? Think about doctor's offices, traffic jams, and checkout lines at the grocery store. Maybe those situations don't cause too much stress. What about when you're waiting on test results or counting down to vacation? Life is full of waiting, and if we don't wait well, it can slowly steal our joy.

The disciples were all huddled in the upper room, having a meal with the miracle-working, crucified, yet risen Jesus. Suddenly, everything makes sense. Everything Jesus said would happen has happened. Can you feel the excitement? Can you see them on pins and needles anticipating their next assignment? And Jesus says, "Wait."

Sometimes we lose joy when we attempt to rush ahead of God's perfect timing. We're all waiting on something; let's take a deep breath and become people who wait well.

Teach me to see the joy in waiting, Lord. Help me to be still and to wait with an attitude that honors You.

Joy in What Really Matters

Enjoy prosperity while you can, but when hard times strike, realize
that both come from God. Remember that nothing is certain in this
life.

—Ecclesiastes 7:14 NLT

Upon returning from a year-long deployment, a soldier spends his first week at home hugging his wife and kids a dozen times each day.

A distance walker recovers from knee surgery and laughs with glee when she's released from her crutches.

Your washer is finally fixed after going on the blink a month ago, and you spend thirty minutes gushing about the joys of plumbing.

We take great joy in things we once took for granted when we're forced to do without them for a time. Suddenly we see them differently; we realize their true value. They fill us with joy in a way they never did before. Have you ever considered that this might be the reason God occasionally allows you to do without certain things (or even people) for a time? When He puts distance between you and the gifts He gives, you realize what really matters in life, and you're reminded that He gives you countless good things every day.

May I recognize the value in everything and everyone You've
given me, Lord, and help me to be patient and grateful when you
temporarily distance me from those blessings.

The Joy in the Bothersome Things

Now we see things imperfectly, like puzzling reflections in a mirror.
—1 Corinthians 13:12 NLT

Have you ever realized that a particular "little thing" ended up making a big impact? Maybe you made a habit of reading at least one book to your child every day, and now she's a voracious reader who pulls straight As in English class. We could say, "Enjoy the bothersome things in life, for one day you'll look back and realize they were the precious things."

When you read the word *bothersome*, maybe you think of running from your car into the store during a rainstorm, watching your kids make a mess as they eat breakfast, or helping your brother change the alternator—again. But when wear, tear, and age take their toll and your legs don't work the way they used to; or once the kids have moved away; or after your brother has joined the military . . . then you realize these annoyances were actually treasures.

Do your best not to miss the little things *or* the bothersome things. Extract the joy to be found in each of them.

Lord, forgive me for looking right past the treasures to be found in the moments that tend to annoy me. Open my eyes to what's really taking place.

See People

She gave this name to the Lord who spoke to her: "You are the God who sees me," for she said, "I have now seen the One who sees me."
—Genesis 16:13

ife is just plain difficult, isn't it? It's very easy to become so focused on the drama of the day that we don't see anything beyond our own issues. We would never verbalize it, but we live in a way that says, "Every man for himself!" We strive to make our lives easier, and meanwhile our brothers and sisters are drowning in despair all around us.

A surefire way to increase our joy is to begin truly seeing other people. Whether we're at the grocery store, the workplace, or our homes, let's put down our phones and lift our heads. When we begin seeing people the way God sees people, we will find ourselves loving them the way He loves them. When we begin loving people, we will reap the joyful rewards.

Many people around us are desperate to be seen. Let's have eyes that see them.

I know I can find joy in truly seeing the people You have placed in my life, Lord. May no one cross my path unseen.

Show Up

When Job's three friends . . . heard about all the troubles that had come upon him, they set out from their homes and met together by agreement to go and sympathize with him and comfort him.

—Job 2:11

Have you ever wanted to live in your own little bubble away from the world for a while? There's just so much stuff out there, right? It's tempting to create our own sanitized version of the world and never venture beyond the four walls of our home. But that's not the way we were created to live. Trying to protect ourselves from any discomfort is unsatisfying.

Job's three friends could have stayed in the comfort of their own homes and simply felt sorry for him. They could have remained surrounded by their own families and thought, *Glad that didn't happen to me.* The problem with that is God's people will never know joy when they ignore the pain of others.

We can discover joy when we are present in someone else's pain. When we make up our minds to leave our homes, to be inconvenienced and uncomfortable, an unexplainable joy floods the soul. Who needs you to show up?

It's easier, Lord, to feel sorry for someone from afar, but I'll find a deep, abiding joy in showing up. Make me someone who shows up.

Motives Matter

Therefore, whether you eat or drink, or whatever you do, do
everything for God's glory.

—1 Corinthians 10:31 HCSB

Have you ever done a good thing with a bad attitude? No doubt most of us have, only to discover that there isn't any joy in doing things that way. When we do a good deed and immediately turn to God and say, "Did You see that? I didn't want to do it, but I did. I listened to her problems even though I have plenty of my own," we do the seemingly right thing, but on the inside we're grumbling and complaining.

We will only have joy in the things we do if we are doing them for the glory of God. Every "good" thing we do for someone should be done with a mindset of pointing that person to the Lord. When we begin acting with godly motives, we will experience the joy that comes with it.

Think about the last good deed you did for someone. Did it bring you joy? If not, ask God to reveal your motive behind doing it.

Give me a heart that seeks to bring You glory, Lord. That is the only
path to a joyful life.

Lighthearted and Joyful

I pray that your hearts will be flooded with light so that you can understand the confident hope he has given to those he called.

—Ephesians 1:18 NLT

odern mind-sets have drained the joy right out of some people's lives. For example, there was a time when people saw the value of rest and sleep and peaceful Sunday afternoons, but no more. During the last generation or so, we've swallowed the idea that the chaos of a hectic schedule isn't just acceptable, it's admirable, and anything less is a sure sign of laziness! In fact, sometimes we're tempted to tell others we're busy even when we're not, as though busyness were a virtue. We end up making excuses for (or even feeling embarrassed about) taking time off to rejuvenate.

How sad that we're so accustomed to feeling stress that we no longer know what it's like to be lighthearted and full of joy. In fact, some of us haven't experienced lightness of heart since we were children. No wonder Jesus encouraged His followers to "become like little children" (Matthew 18:3).

Today, take time to stop and rest until you feel lighthearted and joyful.

Lord, teach me to be like a child; please give me joy and lightness of heart.

Joyfully Passionate

The God who spoke light into existence . . . is the very One who sets our hearts ablaze.

—2 Corinthians 4:6 VOICE

One of *Merriam-Webster*'s definitions of the word *passion* is very fitting for Christians: "intense, driving, or over-mastering feeling or conviction." Believers who truly make a difference for the kingdom of God have strong convictions that drive them carry out God's plan for their lives in their little corners of the world.

Many unbelievers assume that the God-life is boring and stifling, but when we follow God where He leads, it's anything but. Yes, we'll have seasons that are predictable, but we also can't forget that Jesus walked on water during windstorms during His thirty-three years on earth. People of passion find joy in following this same Jesus into the unknown. The musician Andrea Maria sings about having a full life full of passion because this is how God made you to be, so you should let this life unfold just as He planned. Ask God to stir up the passion He put inside you, and see if you don't experience a deeper level of joy.

Lord, stir up the passion in me to do Your will! As the Scripture says, set my heart ablaze.

The Joy of Parenthood

Teach a child how to follow the right way; even when he is old, he will stay on course.

—Proverbs 22:6 VOICE

Joy dissolves when we stop living with a sense of purpose. We all need to know that our lives are about something (or more accurately, Someone) far bigger than we are. *How can I live like that,* you might wonder, *when I'm raising three kids under the age of six? Most days, my life's about sippy cups, cookie crumbs, and keeping my children from climbing on the kitchen counters.*

When God assigned you to parenthood, He didn't withdraw your chance to live a life of profound meaning. But your perspective might need to be adjusted. Ask Him to help you tune in to your higher purpose. For example, your main goal might be to raise your children to become productive members of society—*or* you can acknowledge that you've been given the chance to equip three human beings to impact hundreds of other people. Your influence on them could reverberate into eternity!

Take joy in the truth that one day your cookie monsters could change the world.

Lord, thank You so much for my children, and for those many "routine" days that are shaping them into adults who could impact the world for Your name's sake.

The Weak

Blessed are those who have regard for the weak; the LORD delivers them in times of trouble.

—Psalm 41:1

ave you ever noticed that, when He walked on earth, Jesus seemed to migrate to people who were poor, sick, emotionally troubled, or spiritually confused—in other words, the weak? Several times He was even chided for associating with "sinners." On one occasion, His answer to His accusers was, "I have not come to call the righteous, but sinners" (Luke 5:32).

In like manner, God calls us to minister to those who are weak, such as "orphans and widows" (James 1:27). In the above quote from Psalm 41, He calls those who help the weak "blessed," and adds that He "delivers them in times of trouble." Not only will He bless those who help the needy, He'll also grant them extra protection!

If you've never visited the sick or the imprisoned or served at a free dinner for the hungry, isn't it time you did? Many people who have ministered to the poor have walked away amazed at the joy this gave them. Give, and you will receive!

Jesus, You came to earth to seek and serve the weak and the lost. It's because of Your great love that I'm saved. Praise You!

Forgiven

I said, "I will confess my transgressions to the LORD." And you forgave the guilt of my sin.

—Psalm 32:5

When you forgive someone after he or she has offended you, do you then forget the offense? Or do you bring it up again and again, hoping to make that person feel sad or guilty?

Imagine if God were to store your offenses in the back of His mind, and then bring them up every time you asked Him for something. How would that make you feel? Fortunately, when God forgives, He casts our transgressions "as far as the east is from the west" (Psalm 103:12). Since the east and the west will never meet, that's about as far away as one could toss anything! Along with the sin itself goes 1) the punishment due, 2) the guilt it causes, and 3) the shame you feel. Gone. All of it. God never does anything halfway; therefore, when He forgives, He forgives completely.

Because your forgiven sin is completely gone and forgotten, you have no reason and no right to dredge it up again. Therefore rejoice in God's forgiveness, and make a clean start.

Lord, when You forgive my sin, You wipe my slate clean. Thank You for a new start.

No Room for Shame

Repent, then, and turn to God, so that your sins may be wiped out, that times of refreshing may come from the Lord.

—Acts 3:19

How good do you feel when you know you've done something wrong? Do you try to sweep it under the rug and carry on with life? Most believers have discovered that trick doesn't work. We will never experience joy while living in disobedience to God. The more we try to hide our sin, the more our joy turns to guilt and shame.

The enemy would love for us to just live that way, but God wants so much more for us. There is no place for shame in our hearts, but we have to choose to release it. We can turn away from our disobedience and turn to God. When we do that, He wipes the shame away and fills our hearts with a fresh joy.

What have you been trying to hide? It's time to lift the rug and let it out. There is nothing too big for God to forgive. Don't let it stand in the way of you living joyfully.

Forgive me, Lord, for the things I've done that are contrary to Your will. Please wipe them away and replace my shame with joy.

Thoroughly Equipped

So that the servant of God may be thoroughly equipped for every good work.

—2 Timothy 3:17

Is there anything more frustrating than finding out in the middle of a project that you don't have the right tools? Have you ever tried to prepare a meal only to discover you're missing an ingredient? Whether you're new to a job or a first-time parent, it's very disheartening to feel ill-equipped.

Now think of a time when you excelled at a task. Perhaps you aced a project at school or you delivered an exceptional work presentation. Joy comes when we are thoroughly prepared and able to do something well.

God has set you up for success. In His Word, He has given you everything you need to do what You're called to do. By studying Scripture, you can have the joy that accompanies a servant of God.

I want to be thoroughly equipped, Lord. Keep me in Your Word so that I am prepared to do Your will.

JUNE

Quiet Down

Lead a quiet life: You should mind your own business and work with your hands, just as we told you.

—1 Thessalonians 4:11

Does your life ever seem just a little too loud? Do you ever look around and wonder how it got so crazy? Life can become overwhelmingly loud without a person even realizing it's happening. The constant noise can add undue stress and can slowly drain your joy. Noise can enter your life a number of ways. Being too busy or too concerned with others, affairs are just a couple of them. Often all it takes to restore joy to your life is to learn to quiet down.

In his letter to the Thessalonians, Paul described a life that was pleasing to God. He talked about living a holy life, loving one another, and learning to live quietly. What would it look like for you to live quietly? Perhaps you would need to say no to some things. Being still doesn't come naturally to everyone, so maybe you would have to work on that.

Learning to be present in the moment without trying to plan or predict the next moment will reduce the noise and bring more joy into your life.

Teach me to be quiet, Lord, so that I can better sense Your presence and experience Your joy.

With Joyful Songs

For the LORD your God is living among you. He is a mighty savior.
He will take delight in you with gladness. With his love, he will calm
all your fears. He will rejoice over you with joyful songs.

—Zephaniah 3:17 NLT

Think about your favorite song. How do you feel when you hear it? It doesn't matter if you're an experienced soloist or an only-in-the-shower singer, music speaks to everyone. Something in human DNA responds to music, which is the reason you can probably remember your favorite tunes from high school but can't seem to recall why you walked upstairs.

While studies have been done on the correlation between music and mood, the connection was made long ago in Scripture. Zephaniah gave an image of a God who finds joy in singing over His people with joyful songs. The psalmist felt comforted by a God who would surround him with "songs of deliverance" (Psalm 32:7). Paul and Silas sang while in prison, and the heavenly beings never cease their singing in heaven (Acts 16:25; Revelation 4:8).

Even if you don't consider yourself a musical person, try adding some music to your day. Whether it's gospel or Gershwin, God can cause the melodies to bring joy to your soul.

I love that You are a God who sings. Fill my heart with joy, Lord, so
that I can sing along.

Open Your Home

Show hospitality to one another without grumbling.

—1 Peter 4:9 ESV

D o you know people who possess the gift of hospitality? Their guest rooms feel like a sanctuary, they have an open-door policy, and they are always having company for dinner. Meanwhile, you hold your breath when someone rings the doorbell and pray they don't hear your television and know you're home.

While some may have the gift of hospitality, we all have the scriptural command to be hospitable. In Paul's letter to the saints in Rome, he listed hospitality as one of the marks of a true Christian (Romans 12:13). Peter instructed his readers to show hospitality even though they were all living in exile (1 Peter 1:1)!

Using what you have—whether a lot or a little—to minister to others will always bring you joy. If you're living the life you always dreamed of, or if you wonder where it all went off track, showing hospitality is still the Lord's will, and there is always joy for those obedient to His will.

Open my eyes to opportunities to be hospitable, Lord. Remind me that it's not about showing off; it's about showing You.

Become a God Pleaser

For am I now seeking the approval of man, or of God? Or am I trying to please man? If I were still trying to please man, I would not be a servant of Christ.

—Galatians 1:10 ESV

Some people try to please everyone. The problem with this desire to live a people-pleasing life is that there isn't any joy in it. It may seem, on the surface, that wanting everyone to be happy is a good thing. The problem is—as the saying goes—you can't please everyone because you're not pizza.

Thankfully, there *can* be joy in living a life pleasing to God because it *is* possible to please Him. God's expectations never change. He makes His will known through His Word. No one has to wonder if he or she is loved or accepted by Him. It doesn't take perfection to please Him; it takes only a pure heart.

For everyone caught up in the need to please people, it's time to get off the crazy train and experience the joy of seeking the approval of God. That is the only approval a servant of Christ needs.

Lord, set me free from the need to please people. There's no joy apart from a life that's pleasing to You.

Misplaced Expectations

So the man gave them his attention, expecting to get something from them.

—Acts 3:5

At some point, every person fails to live up to the expectations of others. In the case of Peter and John in the book of Acts, they offered healing to a beggar who was hoping for money. The man got far more than he expected so the story ended well, but many times it doesn't.

All too often people are left disappointed and disillusioned because they expected something that someone was simply unable to give. Those disciples, for instance, could not give that beggar gold or silver because the Lord had specifically told them not to take any on their journey (Mark 6:8). We will greatly increase the joy in our lives when we stop expecting people to provide us with the things our souls need.

We can expect the Lord to do the things we need Him to do. We can lay our requests before Him and wait expectantly and joyfully, knowing He hears and will answer. Those expectations are never misplaced.

I will never find joy, Lord, when I expect people to be and do what only You can be and do.

Free Samples

For it is by grace you have been saved, through faith—and this is not from yourselves, it is the gift of God.

—Ephesians 2:8

Imagine the joy a teenager might feel upon receiving a new wardrobe the day before heading off to college. And imagine the joy her parents would feel to be able to give such a wonderful and essential gift. The best thing the recipient could do is accept the gift, express gratitude to her parents, and share the good news with her friends. There wouldn't be much joy for either the givers or the recipient if she had to figure out how to earn the gift or pay her parents back.

In the same way, salvation through Christ is God's gift to each person. There is nothing we can do to deserve such a lavish gift, and were we were to try, we'd come up woefully short. To live joyfully, a person needs to accept the gift of salvation, express gratitude, and share the good news with everyone. Don't let anyone go through life not knowing about the gift of grace through Christ.

Forgive me, Lord, for the times I've tried to earn or acted as if I deserved the gift of grace. I joyfully accept it and will share it with everyone.

Sunshine

The path of the righteous is like the morning sun, shining ever brighter till the full light of day.

—Proverbs 4:18

Have you ever strolled along a country path, delighting in the glorious sunshine, your spirits high and all your troubles "gone with the wind"? At the end of your walk, your very soul seemed refreshed, your joy was renewed, and you felt ready to face the world once again.

We humans are very sensitive to the moods of nature. Even scientists admit that the weather—especially sunshine or clouds—can affect our moods, even our health. The worst of skeptics must agree that a sunny day is far more uplifting to our spirits than a cloudy one.

The author of Proverbs, Solomon, compared the walk of a righteous person with the brightness of the morning sun. He went on to compare the walk of a wicked person to "deep darkness" (4:19). As a righteous person grows in spiritual maturity, said Solomon, his path gets brighter and brighter, until it reaches "the full light of day," which is heaven.

Who can deny that a beautiful, sunshiny day brings joy to the heart and makes the spirit soar?

Thank You, God, for the sunshine. Thank You that it brings me joy.

The Joy of Variety

And God said . . . "Let birds fly above the earth." . . . And God saw that it was good.

—Genesis 1:20–21

ave you ever marveled at the vast variety of birds God created? Some are incredibly beautiful, others are rather drab; some thrive in the arctic cold, others survive in the Sahara Desert; some are bold and feisty, others are shy and reclusive. Yet all have one thing in common: God loves them.

We humans also come in a wide variety. Some are labeled "beautiful," others "plain"; some live comfortably in the noisy cities, others prefer the wilderness silence; some are at their best in crowds, others are loners by choice. We, too, have this in common: God loves us all.

When God created the different people, plants, and animals, He looked at everything and said, "It is good." We can also enjoy the variety in this world, including the differences in people. How boring it would be if every person in the world looked and acted the same! So take joy in people of differing colors, races, cultures, personalities, and even beliefs.

The variety in Your creation is awe-inspiring, Lord; teach me to appreciate and enjoy it.

Juicy Fruit

The fruit of the Spirit is love, joy, forbearance, kindness, goodness, faithfulness, gentleness and self-control.

—Galatians 5:22–23

ou walk into the kitchen on a summer morning to discover that the bananas are covered in fruit flies. You pour a container of just-bought grapes into the colander for rinsing and see that at least a dozen are fuzzy with mold. You've spent ten years trying to figure out how to tell when a nectarine is ripe, but so far you've failed every time.

Fruit has a short shelf life. But the fruit of the Spirit is all good, all the time. It's always fresh, juicy, appealing, and nourishing because it's a product of the Holy Spirit of God. Along with love, peace, forbearance, kindness, goodness, faithfulness, gentleness, and self-control, it springs up in the life of a Christian who's actively growing in faith. In a believer's heart and spirit, in greater and greater measure, joy increases as he or she matures.

Ideally, there's no such thing as a Christian who's always angry, grouchy, or bad-tempered.

Thank You, Lord, for including joy in the fruits of the Spirit. I want more of it in my life!

Joy in Pain

Shall we accept good from God, and not trouble?

—Job 2:10

Poor Job. The devil had secured God's permission to test Job's faith, as long as he didn't kill Job. So he—probably gleefully—attacked Job with every weapon in his arsenal. Job, however, had great faith; he knew that the Lord was greater, wiser, and mightier than Satan. And Job persevered.

In the book of Job, it's made very clear that Job was enduring horrendous pain, both physical and emotional. Through it all, he questioned God and cried out to Him, struggling to understand what was happening to him. Ultimately he submitted to God's sovereignty and "[repented] in dust and ashes" (Job 42:6).

Although it sounds impossible, we, too, can have even a thread of trust in God—and therefore joy. The joy of the Lord isn't a fleeting thing that disappears as soon as trials come. On the contrary, if we cling to the Lord, He'll remain with us. And *His* joy can be *our* strength.

Thank You, Lord, that in times of trials and physical or emotional pain, we can receive strength, and even joy, from You.

Joy in the Mundane Things

They ate and drank with great joy in the presence of the Lord that day.

—1 Chronicles 29:22

In your opinion, when can we feel joy? The above Bible verse tells us that God wants us to feel joyful even as we do the most mundane things, such as eating and drinking. But, you object, this verse doesn't imply that God is telling *us* to eat and drink joyfully! Oh, but it does. If what the people were doing that day was not acceptable to the Lord, they would not have been "in [His] presence."

Frequently heard in Christian gatherings today is this saying: "God isn't legalistic; *we* are." This is very true! Jesus didn't walk around earth with a sour grimace, looking for things to condemn. He went to weddings, visited with friends, laughed at a toddler's antics. Remember, He's so full of love the Bible says He *is* love, and He's so full of joy He *is* joy.

So be joyful in all you do!

In everything I have to do today, Lord, give me a joyful heart!

Service with Joy

Because you did not serve the LORD your God joyfully and gladly . . . you will serve the enemies the LORD sends against you.
—Deuteronomy 28:47–48

You're working diligently at your desk when you need a package delivered to another part of the plant. The transaction is urgent, but you keep putting it off. Why? Because you dread asking the office courier to convey the package. After all, he's a young man with Down syndrome; to you, he's funny-looking and strange-acting and he always has a little bit of drool clinging to his lips. You shudder.

Trying to keep in mind the words of your pastor's sermon last week about serving God, you grit your teeth and flag down the courier. *Please, God,* you think, *help me to be civil toward him.*

Civil? Is that what God asks us to be toward others? If we are to serve Him, we must do so with the right attitude. Treating others as we would want to be treated—with respect and love—is a key way to serve God, and the consequence of that service is joy.

Lord, please forgive me when I try to serve You with a wrong attitude. Help me to be joyful as I serve, that I might in turn receive Your joy.

Dwelling in God

Strength and joy are in his dwelling place.

—1 Chronicles 16:27

In Psalm 91:1 we read, "Whoever dwells in the shelter of the Most High will rest in the shadow of the Almighty." What an encouraging and glorious promise! If we *dwell* in Christ, we live in and for Him, and if we do that, we'll "rest in the shadow of the Almighty." What an amazing place to be.

There's no way around it: in order to be in someone's shadow, we must be very close to him. Therefore, if we live in and for Christ, we'll be very close to Him. What could possibly bring us more joy than that?

How do we live close to Jesus Christ? The Bible describes many ways: studying the Scriptures, praying to Him, worshipping Him, spending time in His presence, loving Him first and then all others, and obeying Him. Will you make a commitment to live close to Christ today?

Lord, thank You that we can know You keep all Your glorious promises. I promise You that I'll live closer to You, beginning today.

Living with Certainty

For to me, to live is Christ and to die is gain.

—Philippians 1:21

For many people, worry is one of the biggest joy stealers they encounter. Can you relate? How joyful do you feel when you're worrying about something? If you were to do a quick search, you'd find that one of the antonyms for *worry* is *certainty*. We tend to worry about things or situations that hold an element of uncertainty.

It may have seemed, to an onlooker, that Paul was in the midst of an uncertain time. Was he going to live or die? Was he going to be set free or not? Paul was able to maintain joy because he had certainty regarding what really mattered.

Paul viewed his every breath as devoted to the gospel. To live meant he would continue honoring Christ with his life. To die meant that he would see Christ with his own eyes. It was a win-win situation. We can live joyfully when we're certain about the things that are most important. To live is Christ and to die is gain.

When I'm tempted to worry, Lord, remind me that there's nothing uncertain about Your love for me.

Creation

In the beginning God created the heavens and the earth.

An easy way to lose joy is to stop noticing the awesomeness of creation. You can know you've lost a little of the awe when all bugs are annoying, falling leaves just look like work, and the weather always seems too cold or too hot. We forget that every part of creation was dreamed up by an awesomely creative God.

Think about the way a pig plays in the mud, a giraffe stretches out its neck, or a flamingo stands on one leg. The Creator thought up those things to make our world a beautiful and pleasant place to live. Creation was meant to bring us joy.

How disappointing it must be to Him when His people fail to enjoy what He has so lovingly designed. Getting out into creation is a great way to begin living joyfully. Whether you spend an hour on a porch swing on a sunny day, observe a starry night, or take a hike through the woods, God can use His creation to brighten your day and bring joy to your heart.

Thank You, Lord, for the joy that is found in Your creation. You are present in everything from the beauty of the flowers to the sound of the rain.

Knowing You Belong

And you are Christ's, and Christ is God's.

—1 Corinthians 3:23 ESV

Have you ever been the odd man out? It's not any fun to feel overlooked or left out. There's a time in everyone's life when he or she is not included or simply doesn't make the cut. Few pains are quite like the feeling that you just don't belong anywhere. Everyone needs to have someone; there's joy in knowing you belong.

All Christ followers can rest assured that they belong. It doesn't matter if one's marital status isn't what he had hoped or if everyone else seems to have more friends. Paul told the Corinthian believers that they belonged to Christ. The apostle John shared a similar sentiment in 1 John 4:4—"The one who is in you is greater than the one who is in the world."

You can live with joy knowing you belong. You are included; you have a place at the table. God smiles when you show up because you belong to Him.

Thank You, Lord, for claiming me as Your own. It's an honor to belong to You.

Be a Burden Bearer

Bear one another's burdens, and so fulfill the law of Christ.

—Galatians 6:2 ESV

It was never God's intention that people strain under the weight of their own burdens. That's an exhausting and joyless way to live. According to Paul, the law of Christ was best fulfilled when people chose to bear each other's burdens. How could you share someone's burden in your home, community, or workplace?

In order to bear someone else's burden, you have to get close to them. You have to keep in step with them as they make their way through a trial. You might also have to loosen the grip on your own problems and allow someone else to step up and shoulder some of the weight.

God's design is that we become an army of people all walking in the same direction, at the same pace, with the weight evenly distributed so that no one stumbles. It's there, in the sharing of the load, that we find an unexpected joy. The joy comes when we're willing to take on someone else's issue and trust someone with part of ours.

I face weariness only when I try to carry my own load, Lord. I want to experience the joy of being a burden bearer.

On Mission

"Therefore go and make disciples of all nations, baptizing them in the name of the Father and of the Son and of the Holy Spirit."
—Matthew 28:19

Miss Virginia is ninety-six years old. She is frail, hard of hearing, and virtually homebound. Miss Virginia is also one of the most joyful people you will ever meet. At nearly a century old, she is still a mighty prayer warrior with a heart that longs for people to know Jesus.

We're all created with different personalities and gifts, but we all have the same mission. We can never experience a joyful life if we neglect that mission. It doesn't matter where we live, what occupation we have, or what our families look like. We are to be sharing the gospel and making disciples.

It's God's expectation that we will always be about our Father's business. There's no age cap or retirement plan. If we want to experience joy, let's get out there and tell someone about Jesus. There's no joy quite like that! Just ask Miss Virginia, who recently witnessed her seventy-two-year-old friend become a believer and be baptized because she's still on mission.

I will live with joy when I remember my purpose. Open my eyes to mission opportunities, Lord, so that I may be about Your business.

God Is in Control

Our God is in heaven; he does whatever pleases him.

—Psalm 115:3

Even if you aren't a control freak, we all like to think we have things somewhat under control. The idea that we're in control brings a false sense of security that we cling to because it makes life seem a little less scary. Unfortunately, at some point, it becomes painfully obvious how little control one person really has in the grand scheme of things.

Attempting to maintain control of everything in life is a stressful way to live. People were never meant to carry that weight on their shoulders. Children have few responsibilities until they get older because a young child can't handle the stress of adult responsibilities. Likewise, we can't handle the stress of God's responsibilities.

God is in heaven and He does whatever pleases Him. He has everything under control. There isn't any fear in relinquishing control; there is freedom and joy. We can let go of the facade of control and rejoice, knowing that God truly is in control.

I'm so thankful, Lord. I have such joy in knowing there's nothing You can't handle.

When Less Is More

He must become greater; I must become less.

—John 3:30

We live in a world where bigger is better, more is never enough, and everyone strives for first place. Someone else always seems to have more, do more, and be more. Satan loves to whisper lies in our ears that lead us to believe that we are, somehow, *less than*.

The constant weighing of less and more wears on a person's soul until all that's left are weariness and discouragement. But the joke is on the enemy because being less is the key to living joyfully. God never intended for life to be some sort of comparison game.

Joy comes when we finally understand it's always been about Jesus. When things go poorly and people want to pity us, we should point them to Him. When things go well and people want to praise us, we should point to Him. Living a life where we choose to become less so that Jesus becomes more brings joy.

I'm tired of trying to become more, Lord. I want the joy that comes from using my life to make more of You.

Handmade

Then the LORD God formed the man out of the dust from the ground.

—Genesis 2:7 HCSB

When was the last time you made something with your own hands? Whether through gardening, woodworking, or sculpting, there's something inherently joyful about working with your hands. You feel a special pride in knowing that you personally crafted something.

Take a moment and think about creation. God only had to speak and there was light (Genesis 1:3). With a mere breath, He scattered the stars across the heavens (Psalm 33:6). Then it came time for His finest creation. He just had to get His hands dirty, and it made Him very happy (Genesis 1:31).

Whether a purse or a plate, handmade items always bring joy to the recipient and the creator. Everything about you was deliberately designed by the Master Craftsman; it brought Him great joy to make you. Fully grasping that concept will bring great joy to your life as well.

Help me to remember, Lord, that "I am fearfully and wonderfully made" (Psalm 139:14). I'll rejoice knowing that I was formed by Your own hand.

Tradition

*He went to Nazareth, where he had been brought up, and on the
Sabbath day he went into the synagogue, as was his custom.*

—Luke 4:16

Think about your favorite tradition—for example, a holiday at a certain relative's house or an annual family trip. Maybe it's s'mores over a fire pit in the fall or a road trip to the beach in the summer. Traditions bring a special kind of joy into a person's life. Many beautiful memories are closely connected to traditions.

After Jesus' time of temptation, He journeyed back to Nazareth. It was the Sabbath, and His family's tradition was to go to the synagogue. This was the beginning of Jesus' earthly ministry so it was surely a special time as He took part in such a special tradition. He would take those memories with Him as He journeyed to the cross.

It's easy to become so busy that traditions fade away without anyone noticing. Bringing them back will restore some good, old-fashioned joy to a person's life. Take that trip, make Grandma's chicken casserole, or sit and watch that favorite movie that everyone has seen a hundred times. Traditions have a way of spreading joy.

*Family traditions are thrilling and precious. It makes me smile to
think You had them too, Lord.*

A Bubble of Joy

I have calmed and quieted myself . . . like a weaned child I am content.

—Psalm 131:2

One of the words for joy in the New Testament is *chara*, which means "calm delight." Sometimes joy will prompt laughter, excitement, or even shouting, but we can't spend every hour of every day in a blissful tizzy. Nevertheless, we *can* live in a "bubble" of joy even when there are groceries to buy, kids to chauffer, or employees to supervise. Brother Lawrence, the seventeenth-century monk who wrote *The Practice of the Presence of God*, knew this well. He spent many years doing menial, tedious jobs such as washing dishes, but he stayed in God's unbroken presence every moment, in every situation. It was said of him, "When the appointed times of prayer were past, he found no difference, because he still continued with God, praising and blessing Him with all his might, so that he passed his life in continual joy."

We can learn a lot from this humble monk. May God grant us "calm delight" as we work, travel, rest, and pass the 1,440 minutes of each day.

Lord, my request today is that You'd teach me the practice of Your presence so I can enjoy the calm delight that's found in life with You.

Joyful Worship

David told the leaders of the Levites to appoint their fellow Levites
as musicians to make a joyful sound with musical instruments:
lyres, harps and cymbals.

—1 Chronicles 15:16

Have you ever attended a church service where the praise and worship time was, well, boring? In many churches, the congregation seems reluctant to join in, singing either very softly or not at all, as if worship is something only the choir is qualified to do. There's no joy, and there doesn't appear to be any true worship.

This is not how God has directed us to worship. We're to worship Him with our whole hearts, with sincerity, and with joy. Several times in the Bible, we're told to "make a joyful noise" to the Lord (Psalm 95:1–2; 98:4, 6; 100:1 ESV). And in the devotion verse, we're told to worship by using a variety of musical instruments.

If you pour your heart out to God during worship time (or even when you're home alone), you'll find your heart being filled with the joy of the Lord.

Lord, teach me to worship You as You want to be worshipped. Let
me be neither disrespectful nor timid in my worship.

The Allure of Joy

A huge crowd kept following him wherever he went.

—John 6:2 NLT

When you are joyful, people are naturally drawn to you. Maybe you're that joyful person to whom others gravitate. They might not even realize exactly why they're so drawn to you; often, the joy inside a believer is extremely attractive to people.

Sometimes the fact that people want to be near you can feel more like a nuisance than a blessing. Especially if you're naturally reserved, it can be exhausting when others constantly come to you for advice, companionship, or even just casual conversation. The key is to remember that what you have is beyond priceless. If you could bottle the joy in your heart, they'd pay an absurd price for it. People are desperate for genuine joy. As much as you're able, share it with them.

Lord, rejuvenate me when I'm surrounded by people and feel drained. Remind me that You are the reason they are drawn to me.

Joy in the Moment

"Pay attention!"

—Isaiah 28:23 VOICE

The next time you're watching a street performer or attending a wedding, look around and count every person who's recording the occasion on his or her cell phone. No doubt you'll see there are more people observing things second-hand than not! The temptation to immortalize a moment is understandable. We all like to watch certain events a second, third, or hundredth time. But sometimes we fail to realize that when we look at everything through a lens, we're not truly engaged. And this diminishes joy.

Think about the delight you feel when you look at a blindingly red rose or a fat, clumsy puppy. Now imagine looking at that same rose or puppy on a television. Not the same thing, is it? When a TV or phone screen lies between you and the thing that's caught your attention, joy is clouded. Authentic joy comes from being fully involved. So the next time you reach for your camera, *stop*. Let someone else email you the video, and luxuriate in the joy of the moment instead.

Lord, forgive me for missing so many joyful moments that have happened right in front of me. Help me to engage with You and others by disengaging from technology.

The Greatest Treasure

I am my beloved's and my beloved is mine.

—Song of Songs 6:3

Saint Augustine wrote that Christians should be full of praise. He was right to believe that we have more cause for joy than any other group of people on earth. It should go without saying, yet we often live like we've forgotten that out of all the wonderful, priceless treasures that are part of life—family, home, friendships, fulfilling work—we possess the greatest treasure of all: Jesus Christ. Not just eternal life, or the promise of heaven, or the confidence that we'll see our loved ones again. All those riches are glorious beyond words, but they pale in comparison to Jesus Himself.

He is ours; we are His. Think about that for a moment. If you're like most people, your brain can't comprehend this truth, but your spirit can, and that's why joy bubbles up from the inside out when you're in His presence. The next time life seems gloomy or tiresome, remind yourself: *I am His and He is mine.*

Lord, please don't ever let me forget or take for granted that salvation and eternal life are mine—but so are You! Alleluia!

Share the Gospel

May we shout for joy over your salvation, and in the name of our
God set up our banners! May the LORD fulfill all your petitions!
—Psalm 20:5 ESV

How excited do you get over someone else's salvation? Being a part of another person's deliverance will fill you with unspeakable joy. It's an absolute gift from God that we get to play a part in His victory plan.

David wrote Psalm 20 to serve as a guide for the people to use when praying for him. He wanted them to be joyful over any victories God gave him. Likewise, the people of God should be overjoyed when He gives someone victory over his or her sins. Someone being set free and becoming a brother or sister in Christ is definitely cause for joyful celebration.

Jesus said there was rejoicing in heaven over one person who repented (Luke 15:10). We can experience that same joy when people around us come to know Christ. It just takes a willingness to be a part of someone else's life and to share the gospel with him or her. Then we, too, can shout for joy.

Thank You, Lord, for allowing me to experience the joy of being a
part of Your redemption plan.

A Genuine Love

Let love be genuine.

—Romans 12:9 ESV

A sure way to add a lot of tension to your life is to pretend to be something you're not. It takes a lot of time and energy to maintain a false persona, and most people don't have an excess of time *or* energy. It never works out anyway. As soon as you pretend to be a boss in the kitchen, someone will nominate you to supply all the cakes for the community bake sale. It's better to be genuine up front and let people know that your cakes are of the grocery store variety.

The same goes for loving other people. You won't find joy in being phony or over the top; a person's true heart will always be revealed. Paul's instruction to believers was simply to be genuine. The reality is that to love genuinely is to live joyfully.

Imagine what it would look like if everyone genuinely loved one another. We'd be able to celebrate one another without bitterness. We could choose grace over grudges. We could link arms and walk through trials together. And we could live joyfully as brothers and sisters in Christ.

Give me a heart for others, Lord. Let my motives be pure, my love be genuine, and my joy be complete.

Be a Person of Praise

My lips will shout for joy, when I sing praises to you; my soul also, which you have redeemed.

—Psalm 71:23 ESV

A person who lacks joy in his life is, most likely, one who has forgotten all that the Lord has done for him. This is a common tactic of the enemy: he loves for people to focus on what's wrong with the world around them. Satan knows negativity can quickly crowd out joy.

If you find yourself in a bit of a joyless rut, take a moment and review the topics of your recent ramblings or meditations. Was there more complaining and grumbling or praise and gratitude? What about your most recent conversation? Did you feel joyful or drained when it was over?

The psalmist knew that the key to living joyfully was to be a person of praise. Our hearts will fill with joy when our lips are full of praise to the Lord for all He's done. Are you feeling low on joy? Take a moment and begin praising God for who He is, and joyful shouts will soon follow!

You're so very good to me, Lord. Convict me when I'm tempted to complain, and make me into a person of praise.

JULY

The Joy of Small Accomplishments

May the Lord our God show us his approval and make our efforts successful. Yes, make our efforts successful!

—Psalm 90:17 NLT

The year is half over! Doesn't it seem as though just a few weeks ago we were celebrating the new year?

Sometimes the realization that time passes quickly can get us down because we haven't accomplished the things we set out to do. Are you struggling to keep your joy because you feel pulled in too many directions and can't seem to accomplish enough? Ticking even one thing off a to-do list can bring relief from the feeling of being overwhelmed by responsibilities.

Bring out your calendar. Then make a list of five or six moderate projects that are waiting for your time and attention: organizing your closets . . . taking the car for an oil change . . . painting the kitchen. Now, find three days in July that aren't yet dedicated. On the first one, write a couple of those chores you jotted down. Do the same for the second day. On the third day, write, "Rest," and spend that day doing as little as possible.

Feel better?

Lord, time passes so quickly sometimes! Guide me and restore my joy as I tackle these small projects. Help me to be successful.

Slow to Anger

My dear brothers and sisters, take note of this: Everyone should be quick to listen, slow to speak and slow to become angry.

—James 1:19

It doesn't take much to set some people off. A difference of opinion over politics, parenting, or pizza can quickly lead to angry words, hurt feelings, and broken relationships. If you've spent any time around an angry person or if you've ever *been* the angry person, you're aware that angry people are not joyful people.

James, Paul (Titus 1:7), and Solomon (Proverbs 15:18; 16:32; 19:11) all warn God's people to be slow to anger. A joyful spirit is a mark of a person who's learned to overlook an offense, to choose grace over a grudge, and to reject every opportunity to be offended. Anger, just like worry, is a choice.

If anger is an issue for you, ask God to help you let it go. There's a beautiful rhythm to a joyful life and it's *quick, slow, slow*. Be quick to listen, slow to speak, and slow to become angry. Then bask in the joy.

I don't want to live an angry life, Lord. Help me to let go of bitterness, forgive old hurts, and live a life of joy.

Pass It On

Now that I am old and gray, do not abandon me, O God. Let me proclaim your power to this new generation, your mighty miracles to all who come after me.

—Psalm 71:18 NLT

What's your favorite story to tell? Does it involve something from your childhood, the birth of a child, or a grandchild's achievement? Chances are that it somehow involves someone you care about or something special that happened to you. Most of us find joy in telling our stories, whether they include tragedy or triumph. We naturally want to pass on what we've learned to those who come after us.

If you've ever sat with a senior citizen and listened to her stories, you've seen the joy that comes from passing on the memories made and the lessons learned. God's people can experience that same joy by telling the stories of God's greatness. The next generation needs to know of His faithfulness to us.

Think about all God has done in your life. It's pretty amazing, isn't it? Someone needs to hear all about it. Get on out there and proclaim it!

I feel great joy, Lord, when I tell the story of You and Your love. It may be an old, old story but it's the best one that's ever been written.

Freedom

Now the Lord is the Spirit, and where the Spirit of the Lord is, there is freedom.

—2 Corinthians 3:17

What currently has you bound? Is it fear, doubt, or worry? Insecurity, guilt, or shame? Perhaps you can't break free from anger over the way someone has wronged you. Are you bound by feelings of unworthiness? Whatever the source of your chains, Christ has come to set you free.

Christ came so that you could experience freedom and the joy that comes along with it. The enemy can't steal your salvation, but he'll do his best to rob you of your joy. Satan wants to see Christians in bondage, and he often succeeds.

Some men and woman walking among us are more imprisoned than those living in prison cells. There are also people behind bars who are free in Christ. Don't listen to the lies of the enemy. Choose to live joyfully—choose to accept, embrace, and walk in the freedom Christ purchased.

I refuse to be bound, Lord, when You've paid such a price for me to live in freedom and joy.

The One Who Sustains Me

Surely God is my help; the Lord is the one who sustains me.

—Psalm 54:4

f you check your *American Heritage College Dictionary*, you'll see that the word *sustain* means: 1) to keep in existence; maintain, 2) to supply with necessities or nourishment; provide for, 3) to keep from falling or sinking, and 4) to encourage. How accurately the psalmist describes the Lord as "the one who sustains me"! He truly does all these things. Another accurate and descriptive title given to God is *my All-Sufficient One*.

Every breath you breathe is totally dependent on God. He's Jehovah Jireh, the Lord your Provider. He holds you in the palm of His hand and keeps you from falling. He encourages you. What more do you need?

We're completely dependent upon our God for everything. Nothing we can do will keep us alive, provide everything we need, or protect us from all harm, and no human being can encourage us as He can. He's our source of all hope and all joy, our "All-Sufficient One." Hallelujah!

Lord God, in You I have life, and hope, and joy. You alone sustain me. Praise Your glorious name!

Identifying with God's Joy

God saw all that he had made, and it was very good.

—Genesis 1:31

Icebergs that tower one hundred fifty feet above the surface of the ocean.

Butterflies that migrate three thousand miles every autumn.

Tiny, blind fish that live so far under the sea, only researchers have ever seen them.

Dandelions, redwoods, rain, snow, coral reefs, and bobcats—God made each one of these creations and a million more. Why? Because it pleased Him to do so. He called each unique creation good, and we can easily conclude that everything God made gives Him joy. Doesn't it stand to reason, therefore, that they would give us joy as well? We're made in His image, encouraged by His own Word to love what He loves.

If you're fascinated by bugs or boulders; if you'd rather spend the day climbing rocks or playing in the snow than anything else, thank God for allowing you to be able to identify with the joy He feels toward creation.

Lord, Your creations are amazing, from plants and animals to planets and stars. What an artistic God You are.

A Joyful Citizenship

We are citizens of heaven, exiles on earth waiting eagerly for a Liberator.

—Philippians 3:20 VOICE

Have you ever met someone whose circumstances indicated that they were pitiful and destitute, yet they clearly considered themselves to be among the most blessed people on earth? No doubt they'd been transformed by joy.

Author Francis Chan tells a story of a man named Clayton who was suffering from a fatal condition. While documenting his story, various film crewmembers ran into one difficulty after another. Everyone was overstressed and irritable except Clayton, who sat calmly, smiling and humming. "Look, I feel sorry for you guys," Clayton explained later, "because you don't live like this could be your last day." He saw the imminence of death as the promise of heaven—a joy and a gift. His heavenly perspective enabled him to squeeze every ounce of joy out of each situation, no matter how ordinary. He was still on earth, but he understood that he was a citizen of heaven better than those around him.

Oh, the joy of those who know they're "exiles on earth" waiting for their Redeemer!

Lord, I pray that You'll increase my awareness that I'm far less a citizen of earth than of heaven!

Interpreting Your Circumstances

Taste of His goodness; see how wonderful the Eternal truly is.
Anyone who puts trust in Him will be blessed and comforted.
—Psalm 34:8 VOICE

Over the weekend, two friends attended the same wedding, but on Monday when you ask each one what it was like, you're positive they ended up at two different events.

"It was awesome! The bride had an adorable fit of giggles in the middle of the ceremony, the sun shone all day, and the buffet was an adventure in foreign food."

"It was a disaster! The bride acted like a fool, the wind messed up everyone's hair, and the two families couldn't agree on what kind of food to serve."

No one can escape the fact that life holds both sorrow and joy. We can't choose to avoid all suffering, because it simply won't happen that way. However, we can (and continually do) choose what to focus on and how to interpret the million little happenings of a typical day. You can find something to complain about *and* something to celebrate in nearly every situation. One interpretation will make you miserable, the other will bring joy. The choice is yours.

Help me, Lord, to interpret my circumstances through the filter of
Your love and joy.

Joyfully Ordinary

Now you are the body of Christ, and each one of you is a part of it.
—1 Corinthians 12:27

An unseasonably warm, sunny day in the middle of a dreary stretch in January gives us more joy than the one in the middle of summer because it's rare and unexpected, offering a reprieve from the cold. But the warm, sunny day in July is just as crucial. Why? Because without a string of such days, there would be no such thing as summer. Each hot July day is a valuable component of the summer season as a whole, whether we appreciate it or not. And where would we be without summer?

Do you feel completely unexceptional, like a hot day in July? Do you feel a bit lost among peers who are leading lives much like your own? Don't believe for a minute that you're anything less than priceless. Take joy in your role even if it goes unnoticed compared to those that are more unusual or celebrated. Your job in the kingdom might be ordinary, but without you, and the many other saints who feel a bit ordinary, there would be no church.

Thank You, Lord, for the role You've assigned me. May I do it with joy, alongside my many brothers and sisters in the church.

Rejoice with the Rejoicing

Rejoice with those who rejoice; mourn with those who mourn.

—Romans 12:15

How many people do you know? There are people in your family, your workplace, your school, and your community. You bump into folks at the grocery store, the dry cleaner, and the mall. People are all around you! Have you ever wondered how God is at work in their lives?

If we follow the scriptural command to rejoice with those who are rejoicing, we always have a reason to rejoice. There will be seasons when things in our lives are not ideal. The secret is to learn to ask others, "What is God doing in your life?" By turning our attention to the people around us, we'll be able to see God at work in the lives of others and rejoice.

If we're solely focused on our own circumstances, we'll eventually find ourselves running low on joy. But if we learn to see God at work around us, the opportunities for rejoicing will be endless.

Teach me to be a person who's so invested in the lives of others that I truly rejoice when they rejoice, Lord.

He Speaks

The LORD came and stood there, calling as at the other times, "Samuel! Samuel!" Then Samuel said, "Speak, for your servant is listening."

—1 Samuel 3:10

ow does it feel when someone ignores you? Have you ever had a relationship where you were always the one making contact? A person doesn't feel very important or valued if the communication only goes one way.

On the other hand, how special do you feel when someone takes the time to call you by name and speak to you? As believers, we have the privilege of communication with God Himself. It's not one-sided, and He never ignores us or tunes us out.

We find joy in knowing that God takes the time to speak to us and that He doesn't give up on us. We just need to be faithful to listen because our God is faithful to speak. Think about the joy that comes when you spend time in intimate conversation with a dear friend. Now, imagine the joy that will come if you will take the time to listen to the God of the universe speak.

I want to be so close to You, Lord, that I will hear even the slightest whisper from Your heart to mine.

One True Friend

"I do not call you slaves anymore, because a slave doesn't know what his master is doing. I have called you friends, because I have made known to you everything I have heard from My Father."

—John 15:15 HCSB

One of the greatest joys in life is the gift of friendship. To have someone who's on your side no matter what can make all the difference during difficult times. It doesn't matter how many friends you have or how long they've known you. The intimacy and depth of the relationship is what matters.

If you've ever felt like the odd man out or as if you've missed out on the gift of one true friend, Jesus has great news: He declares Himself your Friend. Can you even comprehend that? The Word, the Bread of Life, the Living Water, the Son of God looks at you and says, "I call you My friend."

Perhaps you've read a verse like Proverbs 18:24 and thought, *I don't have a friend like that.* If you're a follower of Christ, you do and it's Christ Himself! Jesus is that friend "who sticks closer than a brother," and that should bring you great joy.

I'm so grateful You've called me friend, Lord. Thank You for Your beautiful gift of friendship.

Family

God places the lonely in families; he sets the prisoners free and gives them joy.

—Psalm 68:6 NLT

It was never God's intention that anyone "do life" completely alone. While we know that God is always with us, it is also important to have people to care about us and to share our lives. Scripture tells us that our God sets the lonely in families.

Sometimes we miss the joy of family because it doesn't look the way we expected it to look. For the person without a mother, God can place an older woman in his or her life to give comfort and wisdom. For the unmarried, family may look like a group of friends gathered around a table, laughing and doing life together.

Life doesn't always (or ever) look the way we thought it would, and neither does family. A family's members may come through biology, adoption, or the bonds of friendship. To live joyfully, we must learn to see that family can come in many forms and to embrace the beauty of the unexpected.

Thank You, Lord, for the beautiful gift of family, no matter how it comes to me. Open my eyes to unexpected blessings.

He Is Near

The LORD is near to all who call on him, to all who call on him in truth.

—Psalm 145:18 ESV

Have you ever, in the midst of a painful time, been unable to see God? Even Job felt that way during those dark days of loss (Job 23:8–9). He was actively seeking some sign that help was on the horizon, and he saw none.

The feeling that God has abandoned you is just a slight of hand; it's a magician's trick. Satan is trying to play "now you see Him and now you don't." Don't be fooled, because God is *right here*. He's as close as your next breath. Even in the midst of unspeakable pain, Job knew this to be true (Job 23:10).

We can have joy during the hardest times because we know that God is near to those who call on Him. We don't have to see Him with our eyes to know He's closer than we can even fathom.

Let's not fall for Satan's worn-out tricks; let's rejoice knowing that God is near.

I will rejoice in the knowledge that You never let go, Lord. You're always near to those who call on You in truth.

Joy and Glory

They raise their voices, they shout for joy. . . . Give glory to the LORD.

—Isaiah 24:14–15

The word *glory* means great beauty, magnificence, and splendor. We've all heard that we should bring glory to God. But have you ever wondered how a person actually does that?

God is already as glorious as He can be. He's *infinitely* beautiful, magnificent, and full of splendor. If He were able to increase in glory, that would mean He's less glorious than He will be in the future—and God is not "less" anything! Even so, we can bring Him glory by sharing stories and testimonies of His love and excellence with other human beings who don't yet know Him. When we "brag" about God, we bring Him renown. Through our words and actions, we can cause others to want Him, to respond to Him, and to seek Him. That brings Him glory. And all the while, as we magnify Him (make Him "larger" in the eyes of others), He grants us joy.

Lord, I want to point everyone I meet toward You so they seek You and You receive glory.

A Word About Perfectionism

It is good to grasp the one and not let go of the other. Whoever fears God will avoid all extremes.

—Ecclesiastes 7:18

magine you've spent the last week repainting the sanctuary at your church. You took care to apply two coats so it would look fresh and clean. You chose beautiful colors and spared no expense on quality paint. You double-checked your work, and you're confident everyone will be thrilled with the results. But just as you're packing up your paintbrushes, a certain church member stops by. She walks in the door, takes a sweeping look around, and points to a miniscule speck on the wall. "You missed a spot."

This is exactly what it can feel like to be on the receiving end of a perfectionist's observation.

Having an eye for detail can be a great asset. But perfectionism is exhausting for both the perfectionist and everyone around him if he fails to temper it with grace.

If you tend toward perfectionism, resist the urge to burst someone's bubble of joy. Choose to see the effort and love that went into the task instead of the spot that was overlooked.

Rein me in when I demand perfection from others, Lord. Teach me to share their joy and sense of accomplishment instead.

A Lesson in Joy from Paul

I pray that God, the source of hope, will fill you completely with joy.

—Romans 15:13 NLT

They say that the greatest danger when stranded in open water is dehydration. In hot weather, it can set in within just a few hours. If, on the other hand, the water is cold, then hypothermia is the most immediate threat.

Of course, one must also think about sharks . . . and wind and waves . . . and jellyfish.

If someone told us a story of how she spent a night adrift at sea, we'd gasp in horror and fuss over her for the suffering she'd endured. But for Paul, a shipwreck—or stoning or flogging, for that matter—was almost routine. We can honestly say that the person who recorded more about the joy of the Lord in his biblical writings than any other single human being was Paul, and yet he wrote many of his letters from prison, while literally in chains . . . that is, when he wasn't being chased by bandits or enduring sleeplessness, hunger, and thirst (2 Corinthians 11:23–28).

If Paul didn't allow self-pity to steal his joy, how can we?

May I live a life of joy instead of self-pity, Lord! Thank you for the example of Paul and for the beautiful lessons recorded in the Bible.

Shaking Off the Fear of Failure

"Do not fear."

—Isaiah 41:10

You're offered the promotion you've wanted for three years, but instead of joy, you feel panic: *What if I can't do the job?*

You have a unique idea for a book, and you can't wait to get started. But by the end of the first page, you're staring at the monitor in terror: *What if no one wants to read this nonsense? What if I never sell a single copy?*

Here's a question to ponder: Who told you that failure is wrong?

Fear of failure will extinguish joy faster than you can say, "I blew it." We've accepted the lie that failure is always bad, and therefore we should avoid it at all costs. However, as Robert F. Kennedy observed, "Only those who dare to fail greatly can ever achieve greatly." To truly follow God wherever He leads, we must be okay with failing once in a while. Only then will we change the world around us. Today, shake off the fear of failure and welcome the joy.

Lord, thank You for leading me into great adventures. I refuse to be afraid of failing! I choose to be courageous and joyful.

Joy in God's Ability

Nothing is too hard for you.

—Jeremiah 32:17

ave you ever watched someone do something with ease and grace after you'd tried unsuccessfully to do the same thing—for an hour? Maybe you struggled all day to solve a problem that involved math only to watch, amazed, as your spouse unraveled it in mere seconds. Maybe you wrestled all day to move a bulky chair until your neighbor stopped by, saw what you were doing, then picked it up and set it down without breaking a sweat. The most shocking thing about each instance is that the task wasn't *less difficult* for the other person, it was *effortless*.

Most of us would quickly agree, "Nothing's too difficult for God!" But think about it: nothing is even *difficult*. Nothing is too challenging, tiring, or confusing to our God, but neither is it even *remotely* challenging, tiring, or confusing. God has never struggled for a split second to accomplish anything.

Take joy in the truth that that's the God who cares for you!

Nothing is difficult, perplexing, or wearying for You, Lord, and that makes me feel so safe in Your care that I could dance for joy!

What Do You Know?

For I know that as you pray for me and the Spirit of Jesus Christ helps me, this will lead to my deliverance.

—Philippians 1:19 NLT

Have you ever watched someone going through a trial and wondered how they were able to keep their joy? What makes one person able to endure while another seems to crumble under the same weight? Paul was well acquainted with trials and tribulations and yet was a man of great joy.

Paul knew, even while sitting in a prison cell, that the prayers of believers had power and that Christ would bring him deliverance one way or another. This knowledge enabled him to live joyfully while being imprisoned and beaten.

When suffering comes our way, no matter what form it takes, what we know matters. In order to live joyfully in every season we must know God's Word and what it says about His ways, His character, and His love for us. No trial can take away the truths we've hidden in our hearts. On the darkest of days, remind yourself of what you know, and you'll live joyfully no matter the circumstances.

I can live joyfully, Lord, because I know Your Word. Your promises are just as true in the bad times as the good.

Without Him

Without him, who can eat or find enjoyment?

—Ecclesiastes 2:25

Some things are so simple that we try to make them complicated. We think, *There's no way it can be that easy!* Those who have struggled to live lives of joy and fallen short have likely tried too hard and chased the wrong things.

Here's the long and the short of it: there's no joy apart from God. No career success, marital status, fame, or fortune can bring a person joy if God isn't in it. You could surround yourself with your favorite possessions, hobbies, and people, and something would still be missing.

Have you looked high and low, yet still struggled to find joy in your life? All you need is God. All the joy your heart can handle is found in Him. He provides the forever kind of joy that the world can't take away. You can walk in joy when you walk with Him.

I'll never have joy apart from You, God. I'll daily bask in the joy that comes from simply being with You.

No Root of Bitterness

See to it that no one fails to obtain the grace of God; that no "root of bitterness" springs up and causes trouble, and by it many become defiled.

—Hebrews 12:15 ESV

When is the last time you felt a little bitter? The world certainly offers plenty of opportunities to feel that way. Whether it's seeing someone else succeed where you've failed or simply feeling overlooked or unappreciated, there are many times you could allow bitterness to spring up in your soul.

Bitterness is like an aggressive weed that chokes out any other plant in a garden. Nothing good can grow alongside a bitter root. Someone who wants to live a life of joy must keep herself far away from bitterness. Paul warned the Ephesians of the dangers when he told them to put bitterness "away from [them]" (Ephesians 4:31 ESV).

Ask God to reveal any hidden roots of bitterness within your heart that may be stifling your joy. Put it far away from you so that you and those around you can live more joyfully each and every day.

Forgive me, Father, for holding on to past hurts or offenses. I choose to let them go and walk joyfully with You.

Be a Truth Teller

Therefore, having put away falsehood, let each one of you speak the truth with his neighbor, for we are members one of another.

—Ephesians 4:25 ESV

L ife is pretty complicated on the best of days. How much worse do we make it when we get ourselves tangled up in falsehoods? Whether we consider them whoppers or little white lies, the truth of the matter is that it's all deception, and there's no joy in any of it.

To live joyfully a person must, as Paul instructed, "put away falsehood." Our words and actions must be truthful and trustworthy. If we are truth tellers, we don't have to worry about being found out or having the truth come to light. We don't have to concern ourselves with who speaks to whom about anything.

Not only did Paul warn believers against any form of dishonesty, Solomon told us that the Lord "detests lying lips" (Proverbs 12:22). We can never live joyfully while engaging in behavior detestable to the Lord. We must live genuinely if we wish to live joyfully.

Guard my lips, Lord, that I may be a truth teller. Let my life be one marked by genuineness and joy.

Beautifully Broken

He heals the brokenhearted and binds up their wounds.

—Psalm 147:3

What do you do when something's broken? Depending on what it is, you might attempt to fix it. Maybe you discard it without a second thought. You might feel frustrated that it no longer works the way you want it to work. Brokenness can be a real bummer.

Kintsugi is a Japanese art in which broken pottery is repaired with a gold, platinum, or silver lacquer. The brokenness of the piece is highlighted and not hidden; it's celebrated instead of discarded. The brokenness adds more value and beauty to the piece.

It's tempting to want to hide our brokenness and to be ashamed of our scars. In order to live joyfully, we have to understand that Christ makes our brokenness beautiful. He fills in the cracks with His love, and the end result is more precious and beautiful than anything we could have imagined. Immense joy can follow brokenness if we allow Christ to bind us up.

I won't be ashamed of the work You've done in my life, Lord. Thank You for making my brokenness beautiful.

Love Lavishly

*Then Mary took about a pint of pure nard, an expensive perfume;
she poured it on Jesus' feet and wiped his feet with her hair. And the
house was filled with the fragrance of the perfume.*

—John 12:3

Have you ever wanted to do something for someone but
were afraid of what it would cost you? Can you think of
a time when loving someone cost you your reputation in the
community or a relationship with a friend? Perhaps there
was a literal financial cost to your act of love.

Mary knew how to love lavishly. When she entered the
place where Jesus was, she wasn't worried what others might
think as she poured the costly perfume onto Jesus' feet. She
didn't concern herself with the monetary value of the act
of love (John 12:5). Her fragrant sacrifice filled the room.

We can live joyfully when we learn to love lavishly. Let's
love our communities. Let's serve our neighbors. Let our
lives be a pleasing aroma to our God (2 Corinthians 2:15).
Joy will come when we live and love without counting the cost.

*There's true joy to be found in loving lavishly. Thank You, Lord, for
Your example of such love.*

The Cost of Joy

*"The Son of Man came eating and drinking, and they say, 'Here is
a glutton and a drunkard, a friend of tax collectors and sinners.'"*
—Matthew 11:19

Have you ever met someone who was so full of joy that
the people around him were convinced he was up to
no good?

Misery loves company (as do anger, cynicism, and pessimism), which is why more than one joyful Christian has
been the victim of rumors. After all, laughter comes easily
to them. They know how to enjoy good food with gusto.
They remain unflappable during a crisis while everyone
else is wringing their hands. They rarely seem uptight,
and they love "those people"—the poor, the homeless, the
"unlovable." They're boring during a gossip session, quick
to see the best in others, and slow to lash out at even the
most infuriating person.

If you can relate, be encouraged: there was once a Man
who not only spread joy, He *invented* it. He was calm, com-
passionate, and quick to see the best in others. He hung out
with "those people" and enjoyed good food so much they
called Him a glutton. You're in very good company.

*Lord, give me great grace and patience with those who are
suspicious of the joy I have in You. Bless them with joy too!*

Joyful Paradox

"Blessed are those who hunger and thirst for righteousness, for they will be filled."

—Matthew 5:6

A paradox is a statement that's true even though it seems contradictory. When we try to explain this wonderful God we serve, we find that our description is filled with paradoxes: He makes us free when we surrender our whole lives to Him; He requires us to die to ourselves in order to gain life; He teaches us that true wealth is available only to those who willingly give everything away.

Here's another one: the only way to maintain a holy hunger for God is to keep filling up on Him.

When we eat as much as we want of a meal, we say we're full and "more than satisfied." We had an empty spot in our belly, and now it's filled. The satisfaction that God gives us is different. The more we pursue Him, the more He satisfies us, and the more we long for Him! The whole cycle sounds illogical but brings us great joy. To be filled with God while also hungry for God is a wonderful, life-giving, joyful paradox.

Lord, help me to never grow numb to Your presence. Fill me up even as You make me hungrier for You.

The Miracle of Joy

Praise the LORD, my soul . . . who redeems your life from the pit and crowns you with love and compassion.

—Psalm 103:2, 4

To some, the admonition to "be a person of joy" sounds as doable as growing wings and flying. The phrase *Shout for joy!* sounds overused and unrealistic. *You're either happy or you're not—and I'm not*, they think. They've forgotten that true, abiding joy comes from the Holy Spirit, and He's all about doing the miraculous *to* and *through* ordinary Christians.

When we're born again, we don't become better versions of ourselves; we're entirely re-created. That's a supernatural event, but the miracles don't stop there. Even the most cynical, bad-tempered person can become a carrier of joy through the work of the Holy Spirit, who imparts the fruits of the Spirit. Many Christians have had the pleasure of running into someone who was once irritable only to discover that he or she radiated joy after an encounter with God. If joy sounds as unreachable to you as the moon, take heart: you serve a God of miracles.

I trust and submit to You, Lord. Please do a supernatural work in my life. Make me a carrier of joy!

Joy Is Strength

The LORD is my strength. . . . My heart leaps for joy, and with my song I praise him.

—Psalm 28:7

ou're exhausted from helping a friend move on a gloomy day when the sun pops out unexpectedly. Suddenly you're filled with joy, and your strength is renewed. You dive into the next stack of moving boxes with vigor.

You're bored and listless after sorting dozens of files when a favorite colleague walks into the office to check on you. She a joyful woman, and soon you're smiling too. Before you know it, you're tackling the chore with new energy.

"Joy is strength," said Mother Teresa, and she was right: it's a cold, fizzy soda on an August day. It's a gentle downhill slope in the middle of a grueling bike ride. No one understands exactly how it happens—how a genuinely exhausted body or brain can be so quickly and thoroughly rejuvenated by a dose of joy—but we all know it works nearly every time. Be someone else's fizzy soda or downhill slope. Cultivate joy, and then give it away.

Lord, thank You so much for the renewed strength that a dose of joy brings. As the giver of joy, You deserve all the praise.

More Than Conquerors

No, in all these things we are more than conquerors through him who loved us.

—Romans 8:37

When is the last time you felt like a conqueror? It's easy to focus on our failings and forget that we've been given victory over the things of this world. Satan would love nothing more than for Christ followers to walk around with our heads hanging and our hearts heavy. He wants us to believe that we're defeated and forget that, through Christ, we're "more than conquerors."

Whether through beating an opposing sports team or kicking a bad habit, there's joy in victory. In order to walk daily in a spirit of joy, we must remind ourselves that Christ has given us the victory. We don't have to listen to the enemy when he whispers reminders of past failures in our ears.

The next time discouragement or despair attempts to take over your spirit, look into a mirror. Look yourself in the eye and be reminded that you're more than a conqueror, and victory looks really good on you. There's no joy quite like the joy of the victorious.

Thank You, Lord, for the thrill of victory that's mine because of Your love for me. Help me to walk in victorious joy.

Stop Comparing

Not that we dare to classify or compare ourselves with some of those who are commending themselves. But when they measure themselves by one another and compare themselves with one another, they are without understanding.

—2 Corinthians 10:12 ESV

How often do you find yourself comparing your life to someone else's? Comparison seems to be the name of the game these days. It's tempting to compare our incomes, the behavior of our children, and even our talents to those around us.

The problem with this game is that nobody wins. Either you come up short and feel discouraged, or the other person comes up short and you feel prideful. Either way, God is not glorified when we compare ourselves to one another.

Our goal is to keep up with Jesus and not the Joneses. He's the standard by which we live. We're to be seeking the things that are above and not comparing the things that are below. Let's end the comparison game; it'll never lead to a joyful life. We'll begin to experience joy when we're more concerned with how we compare to our Savior than to our neighbor.

Lord, help me to heed the instruction of Paul who said, "Imitate me, just as I imitate Christ" (1 Corinthians 11:1 NLT).

AUGUST

To Know and Believe

So we have come to know and to believe the love that God has for us. God is love, and whoever abides in love abides in God, and God abides in him.

—1 John 4:16 ESV

It's possible to have knowledge of something without that knowledge making any difference in your daily life. You could, for instance, sit down, read a medical journal, find the information interesting, and walk away with knowledge of the topic. But would it change anything about the way you lived your life?

There are two different Greek words used in 1 John 4:16: *ginōskō* and *pisteuō*. The first, *ginōskō*, means to have knowledge of something. In this case, John referred to a knowledge of God's love for His people. But it's the second word, *pisteuō*, that holds a key to the joyful life.

Pisteuō means to have full confidence in or to place one's trust in something. To live joyfully, we must move beyond a mere head knowledge of God's love. We must be fully persuaded that God does, in fact, adore us. We'll be joyful people when we begin to truly believe the love God has for His people.

I know and I believe in Your love for me, Lord. I will live joyfully, fully persuaded that I'm the apple of Your eye.

In the Fire

He said, "Look! I see four men walking around in the fire, unbound and unharmed, and the fourth looks like a son of the gods."

—Daniel 3:25

an you think of a time when you felt all alone in a trial? Have you ever felt, like Paul, that nobody stood with you (2 Timothy 4:16)? This is a discouraging place to be for sure. There's nothing joyful about suffering alone. Knowing that someone stands with you can make all the difference.

There is something that all Christ followers need to understand, which will enable them to live joyfully regardless of their circumstances: we have a Savior who never leaves our side. Christ is with us whether we face a fiery trial (Daniel 3:25) or death itself (Psalm 23:4).

Think about the times you thought you were alone. How would your perspective have changed if you realized that the wave-calming, grave-conquering Messiah was standing shoulder to shoulder with you? This knowledge is key to walking with joy through drought and through storm.

Lord, You're beside me in every fire I face. Thank You for never allowing me to endure a trial alone.

Stay in Your Lane

We, however, will not boast beyond proper limits, but will confine our boasting to the sphere of service God himself has assigned to us, a sphere that also includes you.

—2 Corinthians 10:13

Some troubles and trials come our way simply because we live in a fallen world. Certain people will stand against us when we stand firm on the truths of Scripture. Then there are the hardships that, if we're honest, we bring upon ourselves.

God has assigned an area of influence to each of us. We'll find joy in faithfully tending what has been entrusted to us, whether family, finances, or a specific ministry. The easiest way to lose joy and gain stress is to begin worrying about another person's area of influence or to begin comparing areas.

Solomon advised his people to "know the condition of *your* flocks, give careful attention to *your* herds" (Proverbs 27:23, emphasis added). To live joyfully, we must learn to stay in our own lane, to focus on our area of influence, and to know well the condition of our own "flocks."

I've been guilty, Lord, of focusing on other people's areas of influence. Help me to tend what has been entrusted to me.

A Tight Rein

Those who consider themselves religious and yet do not keep a tight rein on their tongues deceive themselves.

—James 1:26

There isn't a person alive who hasn't spoken out of turn at some point or wished he could unsay something. Much like toothpaste from a tube, the words simply can't be put back once they have come out. Words can cause damage that can't be undone.

Learning to control one's tongue will prevent the regrets and hurt feelings that often accompany hasty words. Solomon felt that there was little hope for a man who was too hasty with his words (Proverbs 29:20). He also warned against being too quick to make promises before God (Ecclesiastes 5:2).

To truly live joyfully, a person needs to heed the instructions given in Scripture. It's often the simplest commands that, when disobeyed, wreak havoc in a life. We can have joy when the words of our mouth are acceptable to God (Psalm 19:14).

Forgive me, Lord, when I've been too quick to speak. May my words bring glory to You and life to those around me.

The Morning Star

"I will also give that one the morning star."

—Revelation 2:28

ave you ever given someone a gift or offered something that you didn't feel was fully appreciated? Perhaps they failed to fully grasp the value of what was being given. Or maybe you've received something and wondered why it was a big deal.

We miss out on a lot of joy by not fully understanding the promises made to us in Scripture. In Revelation, for instance, the church in Thyatira was promised that those who endured and remained steadfast would be given "the morning star." To fully grasp the joy of that promise, you have to keep reading.

At the very end of the book of Revelation, Jesus identified Himself as "the root and the descendant of David, the bright morning star" (Revelation 22:16 ESV). Jesus told His people that, after they endured, they would get Him! There is true joy in digging deeper into God's Word.

I don't want a shallow understanding of Your Word, Lord. Take me deeper and give me joy as I partake of Your promises.

Gifts in the Wilderness

"Therefore I am now going to allure her; I will lead her into the wilderness and speak tenderly to her."

—Hosea 2:14

How quick are you, during a time of trouble, to say, "What have I done to deserve this?" Often our first response is to view our trials as punishment. It's difficult to "rejoice always" when we're in the midst of a wilderness thinking, *Why me?* (Philippians 4:4).

To walk with joy through the wilderness, we must recognize the gifts that are awaiting us. Sometimes God wants to stir up the passion we once had for Him. Other times the wilderness is a place of protection (Exodus 13:17–18). Though the enemy would have you believe otherwise, the wilderness can be a place of provision (Psalm 78:19).

We can have joy in the midst of any circumstance if we train our hearts to look for the gifts. If you're currently in a wilderness, look for the gifts of passion, protection, and provision.

Lord, open my eyes to the gifts in every circumstance so that I can walk with joy wherever You lead me.

Dare to Be Disappointed

Israel said to Joseph, "I never expected to see your face again, and now God has allowed me to see your children too."

—Genesis 48:11

Israel believed that his son had been dead for years. He had no reason to expect to see Joseph's face again on earth. There wasn't much hope for a surprise reunion. It would have never occurred to him to even ask for such a thing. Can you think of something you long for but have never thought to pray about?

A person who lives joyfully always remembers that God goes above and beyond for His people. Has God ever done something for you that caused you to say, "I never expected that"? It makes you wonder what else you may have missed out on (James 4:2).

Many people don't ask for things because they fear disappointment. Longings often come from a tender place within, and we fear the damage one more disappointment would cause. Joy comes when we no longer fear disappointment and bravely ask our God for abundance (Ephesians 3:20).

Thank You, God, for doing more than we could ask for and for being more than we can even imagine.

Breath of God

Your daughter is dead; do not trouble the Teacher any more.

—Luke 8:49 ESV

How many times have you believed that something was dead, hopeless, beyond repair, or not worth the fight? Has the enemy tried to suggest that you shouldn't trouble God with that thing anymore? Whatever it is that you fear is dead—don't believe it.

To live joyfully, you must remember the power of your God. You have a God who breathes on dead things and causes them to live again (Ezekiel 37:13). You have a God who calls dead men from their graves with a mere word (John 11:43). You serve a Savior who walked out of the tomb Himself (Luke 24:2–3).

Nothing is so dead that God's breath can't resurrect it. No hope or dream is so buried that it can't be called forth with just a word. What Satan calls dead, God calls merely asleep. When the enemy says, "Don't trouble God anymore," just wait for God to breathe. Rejoice; God is still in the resurrection business.

Praise You, Lord, that nothing is dead until You declare it so. I will rejoice and wait for You to breathe.

God Still Has a Plan

"For I know the plans I have for you," says the LORD. "They are plans for good and not for disaster, to give you a future and a hope."

—Jeremiah 29:11 NLT

If polled, three out of four Christians would probably claim Jeremiah 29:11 as their "life verse." Some people quote it to every friend going through a trial. It's written on Post-it notes and cross-stitched onto pillows. There's no denying that it's a catchy verse.

The best part of this verse is often forgotten; it was a message from God to a people living in exile (Jeremiah 29:4). They were banished to a distant land, surrounded by unfamiliar territory and unfriendly faces. They were scared and scarred. They were worn and weary. Then, in the midst of their suffering, God whispered hope.

You can take comfort in knowing that God has a plan, and you can find joy in knowing that He *still* has a plan in spite of your mistakes and flaws. When you look around and wonder how you got here, He knows. When your own sin has caused your current pain, God still has a plan. You can rejoice knowing that God's plan is a good one.

Thank You, Lord, that You still have a plan for me. I know that, wherever I find myself, You have hope and goodness in store for me.

Let It Be

Zechariah asked the angel, "How can I be sure of this?"

—Luke 1:18

What do you do when times are difficult? When you've trusted until you're tired and you've endured until you're empty? What's your response when well-meaning folks toss "For those who love God all things work together for good" your way like it's a magic cure-all for whatever ails you (Romans 8:28 ESV)? If you're Zechariah, you say, "Prove it."

It's easy enough to judge him, but who hasn't, at some point, yearned for just a little tangible reassurance? Maybe you're trying to pay your bills from an empty bank account. Or you've been sitting with someone you love, and he or she is fading fast. Sometimes He takes pity on us. He hears our doubts and lets us touch the scars (John 20:24–27).

There is joy for those who are able to believe even when they can't see (John 20:29) and who simply take God at His Word (Luke 1:45). Let's take our cue from Mary and joyfully say, "Let it be to me according to your word" (Luke 1:38 ESV).

Lord, I have been Zechariah more often than not. Please give me joy because of what I have believed.

Touch the Future

With my mouth I will make your faithfulness known through all generations.

—Psalm 89:1

What do you hope to leave behind when you're gone? Most people aspire to leave some mark on the world or some monetary gift to their children. While these things may bring some satisfaction, true joy comes when we successfully pass on our faith. This is the only true way to touch future generations.

Believers are instructed in Scripture to teach their children the Word of the Lord (Deuteronomy 6:7). We are to store up, for ourselves and those who come after us, things of eternal significance (Matthew 6:20). This is vital if we desire the ultimate joy of seeing our children walk in truth (3 John v. 4).

A joyful life is one lived with the future in mind. Let's proclaim His goodness to those who follow us. Let's make sure we're not the reason that the next generation hasn't heard of God's Word and works among His people.

I will proclaim Your Word, Lord, to the next generation. May I have the joy of seeing my children walking in Your truth.

Security

Lord, you alone are my portion and my cup; you make my lot secure.

—Psalm 16:5

Many natural disasters have ripped across America, some causing people to lose everything they own: their photographs, important papers, furniture, vehicles—even their entire homes. How difficult it must be to see your security wiped out in a matter of minutes. But wait! Is their security really gone?

In Psalm 16:5, David tells us that the Lord is our security. Friends, neighbors, and even strangers can donate food, water, clothing, furniture, and money to the victims of disasters, but only God can truly keep us safe, both physically and spiritually. Storms may destroy, banks may collapse, and the enemy, Satan, may attack us, but the Lord assures us, "Never will I leave you; never will I forsake you" (Hebrews 13:5). What greater, more invincible insurance could we have than the same God who created heaven and earth, who placed the stars in the skies and set the planets in motion?

Rejoice! Feel the joy! God, our God, is our security.

Lord, I acknowledge that You, and You alone, are my security. Praise You!

At Peace with Others

Search for peace, and work to maintain it.

—1 Peter 3:11 NLT

This verse tells us to "work to maintain" peace. Interestingly, Romans 12, which is full of brief "nuggets" that explain how to live the joyful life, also tells us to do all we can to live in harmony with others. We can tell from the way the Romans passage is worded that Paul was a realist; he understood that certain folks don't want any part of harmony. Sometimes they've been wounded; they've decided that even the slightest offense is cause for war, which makes peace next to impossible.

Other times, they're not so easily angered, but they thrive on drama: the sky is always falling, and the smallest hiccup becomes a crisis. Often, numerous people are pulled into the drama via breathless conversations and texts, but you have a choice: join in the ruckus, or calmly distance yourself. If you *must* participate, then do your best to defuse the situation. The result is that you'll be able to hold on to joy while living at peace with everyone—including yourself.

Lord, when angry words are flying back and forth, or drama unfolds all around me, help me to be at peace with everyone.

The Joy of Integrity

The Lord... delights in people who are trustworthy.

—Proverbs 12:22

You're in a rush, fumbling through the self-checkout register at your local department store, when you realize that a six-dollar box of coffee pods has accidently rung up for "$00.00." Catching the customer service clerk's attention could take a while, not to mention the hassle of having to explain what happened.

Do you bag the coffee, pay for your other items, and get out of there? Or do you speak up?

The word *integrity* means observing a specific code of values, but it also refers to the state of being undivided. When a Christian lives dishonorably, his allegiance is divided between God and self, and the result is anything but joy. So if you're ever in a predicament like the one described, remember that your integrity is worth far more than six dollars, or six thousand, or a million. In fact, it's priceless. Jesus paid a price far greater than we'll ever understand so we could possess the joy of living a life of character.

Thank You, Lord, for the joy of living with integrity. Help me to grow more and more.

The Joy of Paring Down

God is not a God of confusion.

—1 Corinthians 14:33 ESV

Why is it that some of us have sizable, even impressive, vocabularies but don't know how to say no? We bite off more than we can possibly chew, then end up with a schedule that's exhausting, bewildering, and unmanageable.

Take a lesson from people who know the art of an uncluttered closet. They'll tell you that a cardinal rule to tidy closet-keeping is "When something comes in, something else goes out." For example, you're not allowed to hang those great clearance jeans in the closet unless you first toss a different item into the Goodwill pile. Also important is the periodic purge, when everything you haven't "made friends with" is eliminated. Finally, if it's not clothing-related, it doesn't go in the closet—*ever.* Clothes closets are for shirts and shoes, not Christmas decorations and broken toys.

To maintain joy and throw off stress, treat life like a closet: if you take on a new responsibility, drop an old one. Periodically eliminate anything that's not a good fit, and don't fill your life with activities that don't belong there.

Help me, Lord, to stop taking on more than I can handle. I promise, with Your guidance, to clean out the closets in my life—all of them.

The Joy of the Good Fight

I have fought the good fight. . . . I look forward to what's in store for me.

—2 Timothy 4:7–8 VOICE

You're mindlessly scrolling through your Facebook feed when you see a particular post that makes you cringe. The subject isn't necessarily controversial, but the way it's worded, or the subject matter (animals, child care, exercise) qualifies it as "one of those posts"—you know, the sort that attracts everyone on the Internet who's itching for a fight.

"That's ANIMAL ABUSE!" someone writes in all caps because the sweet puppy is being "forced" to wear a sweater.

"What kind of a parent would let their child do that?" someone scolds, missing the humor of an endearing video.

Each day we're surrounded by a million pointless, worthless debates and arguments, but do you know what Bible tells us about a "good fight"? This fight involves striving for all that's righteous and true. It's worthwhile because it concerns eternal things. Today, don't lose your joy over a meaningless argument; instead, focus on the good fight.

Lord, I want to fight the good and noble fight; teach me which battles matter, and which ones don't.

Every Empty Place

Then the women said to Naomi, "Blessed be the LORD, who has not left you this day without a redeemer."

—Ruth 4:14 ESV

Can you think of a time when you experienced emptiness? Whether an empty seat at the table, an empty bank account, or an empty womb, emptiness can be devastating. The effects of experiencing it can make us unrecognizable to our friends (Job 2:12) and neighbors (Ruth 1:19).

Naomi knew what it was like to be filled with good things, and she knew was it was like to be empty (Ruth 1:21). How is a person supposed to rejoice continuously while walking such a dark, lonely road? There is one promise that holds the key to joy in the midst of emptiness: that of a Redeemer.

Whatever loss or emptiness we experience, we can rejoice knowing that God will restore to us whatever this world has taken (Joel 2:25). Trust Him to redeem it all and to fill in every one of your empty places.

When the emptiness seems more than I can bear, Lord, I will rejoice knowing You are able to redeem and restore.

Great Is Your Reward

"Rejoice in that day and leap for joy, because great is your reward in heaven. For that is how their ancestors treated the prophets."

—Luke 6:23

hances are that everyone has, at some point, been excluded or disliked; this is, without a doubt, a painful experience. How are you supposed to respond when someone ignores or hates you (Luke 6:22)? A natural response would be hurt or anger, but Jesus tells believers to respond quite differently.

When we're left out, ostracized, or persecuted because of our faith, Jesus says we're to rejoice. We're told to leap for joy! Why would we respond in such a way? Our faithfulness to Christ will result in great rewards in heaven; that's how we can live joyfully in the face of rejection or abandonment.

The next time someone walks away or mocks you because of your faith, choose joy over bitterness. Remind yourself that you're experiencing the same thing your forefathers experienced and that the rewards are more than anything you could imagine. Then, if you have it in you, go ahead and leap.

Any rejection I experience on earth will one day fade away. Thank You, Lord, for the joy of a heavenly reward.

Remove the Stone

"Remove the stone," Jesus said. Martha, the dead man's sister, told Him, "Lord, he's already decaying. It's been four days."

—John 11:39 HCSB

There's immense joy in being a part of what God is doing at any given time. What if Moses hadn't reached out and grabbed the snake by the tail (Exodus 4:4)? What if the priests hadn't stepped into the Jordan (Joshua 3:13)? What if the blind man hadn't believed in the power of Jesus (John 9:7)? What if Martha and Mary hadn't moved the stone (John 11:39)?

To live joyfully is to believe that God can do anything. What is God calling you do to? What's that thing that seems ridiculous when you say it out loud? It would be a shame to miss out on a miracle because you feared looking foolish.

We just have to believe. We pray for provision even when we can't see any possible way for it to happen. We pray for relationships to be restored even when renewal seems impossible. We believe in the impossible, and then we rejoice when our Lazarus comes forth.

It's pure joy to see You at work, Lord, and a privilege to play a part in Your mighty plan of redemption.

Places of Waste

*A sound of joy and gladness, the voice of the groom and the bride,
and the voice of those saying, Praise the LORD of Hosts, for the
LORD is good; His faithful love endures forever as they bring thank
offerings to the temple of the LORD.*

—Jeremiah 33:11 HCSB

Have you ever as though the whole day was a waste? Or
possibly the issue is even bigger than that. Maybe you
feel as if you've wasted years. The job you've had for decades is eliminated. A relationship you thought would last
forever didn't. Someone you love leaves this world way too
soon and you think, *What a waste.*

Whatever place of waste you may find yourself in, today
the Lord has a promise for you: there will again be joy and
gladness. There will be times of celebration and cause for
praise because the Lord is good (Jeremiah 33:10–11).

We can know that even if we can't quite see it now, joy
and gladness are coming. God's faithful love endures forever. He makes flowers bloom in barren deserts (Isaiah
35:1) because He's all about restoring what looks to us like
a complete loss. He can take our places of waste and make
them places of joy.

*Lord, I trust You to bring joy and gladness, celebration and praise
to the wasted places of my life.*

It's All Worship

Then God said, "Take your son, your only son, whom you love—
Isaac—and go to the region of Moriah. Sacrifice him there as a
burnt offering on a mountain I will show you."

—Genesis 22:2

We tend to hold tightly to things. Without even realizing it, we sometimes cling more tightly to people, dreams, and objects than we do to God Himself. That's why many struggle with a passage like this one in Genesis where Abraham was called to sacrifice his only son.

Isaac was the long-awaited son of the promise. He'd been longed for and was dearly loved. God instructed Abraham to sacrifice the very thing he treasured most. Because Abraham loved God more than anything else, his life was an act of worship.

We can live joyfully when we begin to view every aspect of our lives as worship. Trusting God with the things and people most precious to us is an act of worship regardless of the outcome. We can rejoice knowing that God is pleased by our trust and obedience.

Lord, I want my entire life to be one long act of worship. May I
never cling too tightly to anything except You.

Seeing People

Then he turned toward the woman and said to Simon, "Do you see this woman?"

—Luke 7:44

What do you see when you look at the people around you? It's pretty easy, especially if we know someone's story, to immediately pick up on a person's flaws or failures. Sometimes when we look at a person, we think of what we've heard other people say about him or her.

When the sinful woman entered Simon the Pharisee's home, he saw her sin (Luke 7:39). He knew who the woman had been and everything she had done, and he judged her for it. Jesus wasn't concerned with what Simon knew but with what he saw. He wanted Simon to truly see the woman.

When it comes to looking at other people, judgment and joy could not be further apart. Judgment sees a person's past, her shame, or her indiscretions. But there's no joy in judgment. Joy comes when we truly see each individual and begin to love the way God loves.

I want to see people the way You see them, Lord. I want the joy that comes when I choose to truly see and love people.

Promise Keeper

For all the promises of God find their Yes in him. That is why it is through him that we utter our Amen to God for his glory.
—2 Corinthians 1:20 ESV

Has anyone ever broken a promise to you? Something happens when people fail to keep their word; we don't get quite as excited when they promise something new. We wait with uncertainty, and we hesitate to get our hopes up lest we are disappointed. *Fool me once, shame on you; fool me twice, shame on me.*

There's cause for joy for believers because every promise God ever made is fulfilled in Christ. When we read a precious promise in Scripture, we can get excited knowing that God has never failed to keep His Word. We don't need to temper our joy because God doesn't disappoint.

Is there something in God's Word that you've been afraid to believe? Is there a promise you long to claim but fear disappointment? Rejoice, believer, because our God is a promise keeper, and every one of His promises find its Yes in Jesus Christ.

Thank You, Lord, for being a God of Your Word. I rejoice knowing that every promise You've ever made will come to pass.

His Name

At the name of Jesus every knee should bow, in heaven and on earth and under the earth.

—Philippians 2:10

Where does your strength come from? Many people rely on their physical prowess or attempt to intimidate with their wit and intellect. If the source of our power is anything other than the name of Jesus, we'll inevitably end up looking weak and foolish.

When it comes time to battle with the enemy, we can rejoice knowing that there is power in the name of Jesus Christ. That precious name is a strong tower where the righteous may run and find safety (Proverbs 18:10). That name is the source of our salvation (Acts 4:12).

We're people of joy no matter how mighty the foe may seem or how immovable the mountain may appear. We can have joy knowing that the power of His name is at work on our behalf, in every situation. Rejoice; every knee must bow at the sound of the name of Jesus.

Jesus, I never tire of the sound of Your name. It brings perfect peace to my soul and immense joy to my heart.

Same Mind

*Complete my joy by being of the same mind, having the same love,
being in full accord and of one mind.*

—Philippians 2:2 ESV

Can you think of anything less joyful than being at odds with someone you care about? Whether a disagreement involves sports, politics, or musical preferences, discord doesn't give anyone the warm fuzzies. Strife steals joy not just from those in a dispute, but also from everyone who cares about the people involved.

Paul was speaking to the Philippian church when he said, "Complete my joy by being of the same mind." He wanted his fellow believers to experience the joy of spiritual unity, and, by doing so, they would complete Paul's own joy as well. Unity among believers is essential for all of us to experience complete joy.

Jesus prayed that we would all be one (John 17:21). Let's complete one another's joy by being of one mind and one mission. If we're all loving the Lord with our hearts, souls, and minds—and loving our neighbors the way we love ourselves—we'll experience complete joy.

Lord, I desire the joy that comes from being in unity with fellow believers. Give me a heart that seeks to have the same love.

Joy in Your Environment

Peace be to you, and peace be to your house.

—1 Samuel 25:6 ESV

As humans, we're very sensitive and responsive to our environment. Everything from the color of our bedroom walls to a slight change in humidity makes a difference as to how we feel, both mentally and physically. (Interior decorators and aromatherapists understand this well!) God designed us this way, so go easy on yourself if you have a rougher time than most during an especially cold or rainy spell.

If you find yourself longing for an environment that's far removed from the one where you spend most of your time, take an active role in changing it if at all possible. If you're pining for a weekend at your favorite mountain cabin, talk to your spouse about spending a hundred dollars on a mini-fireplace for your living room. Aching for some beach time? Fill a corner of your office with a tall tropical plant. Hankering for a hike in the Appalachians? Take the dog to the closest state park and see how quickly you can cover a couple of miles. As much as you're able, make your environment a joyful one.

Lord, please give me creative ideas as to how I can make my environment one that brings joy to me and others.

My Cause

For you have upheld my right and my cause, sitting enthroned as the righteous judge.

—Psalm 9:4

Did you read the above Scripture carefully? Think about it: no matter what happens to us here on earth, no matter how our rights might be trampled or whatever is important to us might be crushed, we can know that eventually God, the Righteous Judge, will hand down *His* ruling, and all human doubters, abusers, accusers, or persecutors will be overruled and punished. When God says we should not seek revenge upon our enemies because He'll be the avenger, He means just that!

What joy we can embrace just by knowing that one day, either here on earth or in heaven, every offense ever committed against us will be avenged by God Himself. We can know that all wrongs *will* be made right! What joy is ours when we know that God's love for us is so high, wide, and deep that He'll correct every wrong ever done to us! God sees and hears our hurts. Trust Him to make things right.

Thank You, Lord, that You that You are my Righteous Judge. Grant me joy as I rest in You.

The Joy of Seeing Clearly

I pray that the eyes of your heart may be enlightened.

—Ephesians 1:18

You don't have to be Sherlock Holmes or Hercule Poirot to uncover evidence of God everywhere you go. His reflection is all around. But sometimes the task of living distracts us so continually from the beauty around us that we stop seeing with "the eyes of [our] heart." And that's when we notice we don't have the joy we used to have.

Are you willing to set aside one hour so the Lord can set you right again? Today, go outdoors for a full sixty minutes. Spend that time walking, camera in hand. (For this experiment, slower is better: no speed walking or running.) Don't go back into your house or workplace until you've snapped ten photos of something beautiful, comical, or intriguing: a delicate weed pushing through a crack in the sidewalk, a teenager zipping by on a skateboard, the setting sun peeking out from behind an office building. You'll be shocked at how easy it is once you slow down and actually see what's all around you.

Lord, please open my eyes so I can take joy again in the evidence of Your presence all around me.

Taking Oneself Too Seriously

A time to weep and a time to laugh.

—Ecclesiastes 3:4

You're taking a seat before the start of a meeting when another attendee walks in the door. His shoe catches on the doormat and he stumbles. Immediately, he curses under his breath and looks around to see who witnessed his embarrassing moment. Before you can scoot across the room to straighten the rug, another man steps through the doorway, and he trips, too. He laughs at himself, bows theatrically, and straightens the rug.

What's the difference between these two men? The angry man takes himself very seriously, and the joyful man does not.

Taking yourself too seriously comes from seeing yourself as very, *very* important. On the one hand, you *are* important; you're priceless beyond measure, and every detail of your life matters to God . . . but on the other hand, you're a flawed, blundering human being apart from the grace of God.

Jesus. The kingdom of God. Serving others.
Now *that's* serious business.

Lord, help me to stop taking myself so seriously so I can get on with the business of living joyfully.

No Regrets

Now choose life, so that you and your children may live.
—Deuteronomy 30:19

You spent months saving and planning for a vacation in the South Seas with your family. Finally, you've arrived—just in time for a late-summer cyclone. Flights back home have all been grounded, so you have two choices: sit in the motel room with the family, all of you grouchy and basking in self-pity; or sit in the motel room with the family, having that picnic you prepared for the beach indoors, playing games, and making memories for your family. Which would you choose?

Life consists of many choices, some very difficult, some no-brainers, but each one requires a decision. Sometimes the decisions we make don't have much of an impact on our lives, but occasionally there's a decision we must make that can determine our futures. In the above dilemma, will you be pleased with the choice you made, or will you regret that choice the rest of your life?

A wise elderly lady once said, "The worst things to have to live with are regrets." A regret-filled life is not a joy-filled life. Make choices that you won't later regret. Choose life!

Lord, forgive me when I choose to wallow in self-pity rather than choosing to "turn my frown upside down." Help me to live a joy-filled life.

Searching the Soul

Search me, God, and know my heart.

We all know that we should brush our teeth at least twice a day. If you ignore your teeth or don't take care of them properly, little problems can soon become big problems. But did you know you should also regularly search your heart? It's easy to do wrong things and be totally unaware of it. By carefully searching your heart each day and asking God to show you where you're coming up short, you can often unearth the "little sins" that could, if uncorrected, soon become "big sins."

Even microscopic particles of food can cause your teeth to decay. Likewise, even "microscopic sins," such as eating too much at a buffet, can cause dry rot in your soul. To rid your teeth of food particles, you must brush them regularly; to rid your soul of dry rot, you must search your heart—regularly—to discover the culprit sin, and then confess that sin to God and repent of it. Nothing brings joy to a person's heart like a clean conscience and a clean soul.

Search my heart, Lord, and show me any hidden sins, so I can confess them and make things right today.

SEPTEMBER

Celebrate

"Three times a year you are to celebrate."

—Exodus 23:14

If you are (or are married to) a Cubs fan, you will well remember the celebrating when the team won the 2016 World Series. Chicago was in an uproar! Even people who were not sports fans were caught up in the fun and gaiety. It was almost like New Year's Eve, with music and laughter and smiles all around.

The fun and celebration of a big win, however, can't compare with the inexpressible joy of heaven. Just imagine that atmosphere: no pain, sickness, worries, stress, hurt feelings, traumatic memories—and no taxes! In fact, God Himself "will wipe away every tear" (Revelation 7:17).

When we believe in God and an afterlife, we have hope, and hope brings joy. Celebrating is temporary and superficial; joy is lasting and life-changing. There's nothing wrong with celebrations—Jesus even went to dinners and wedding feasts. But celebrations depend on the environment. An accident, illness, or even an argument can spoil the whole party. When we feel the joy of the Lord, however, it can and often will last, no matter what's happening around us.

Thank You, Lord, that knowing You fills my heart with hope and with joy.

Joy Forever

You will inherit a double portion . . . and everlasting joy will be yours.

—Isaiah 61:7

Think about a time when you experienced pure, undiluted joy. Maybe you were sledding with your kids during the first snow of the year. Maybe you were surrounded by your church family, singing your heart out during a worship service. Or perhaps you were by yourself, floating in a clear, blue swimming pool with nothing else to do on a lazy Saturday. Can you remember the feeling of bliss? Of having absolutely no worries, no weight on your shoulders?

Now think about what it felt like to have to come in, take off your snowsuit, and get ready for bed—or what it felt like when the service ended, or you had to finally get out of the pool. When you had to go back to "real life."

One day, you'll be looking at an eternity of nothing but joy like you felt that day, times a thousand. The reason—the *only* reason—is because you'll be forever with God. Unending bliss: one day, *that* will be "real life."

It's hard to imagine, Lord, what it'll be like to feel pure joy for eternity, but sometimes I can barely wait!

Joy in the Work

The LORD your God will bless you in all your harvest and in all the work of your hands, and your joy will be complete.

—Deuteronomy 16:15

How often we do not feel like working! Relaxing or having fun seems like a better way to while away our hours. However, the Bible tells us that we'll find joy in the satisfaction of our work. Even if we don't particularly like the job situation, some of our coworkers, or perhaps the work itself, if we do our best at all times we can feel fulfilled—and, yes, even joyful—by producing a job well done.

God created us to be productive. He wants us to experience the same joy He feels when He creates by doing our work efficiently, with dedication, commitment, and integrity.

If we do our work sloppily, or perhaps well but with a sour attitude, that's not pleasing to God because we're not working in accordance with His will. If we defiantly refuse to do our work well, we won't find the joy of the Lord in what we do. Always do your best!

Forgive me, Lord, when my attitude toward work is not in accordance with Your will. Teach me to always do my best.

My Fortress

The LORD Almighty is with us; the God of Jacob is our fortress.
—Psalm 46:11

I n biblical times the strongest protection against an enemy was a fortress. In the Bible, God is compared to a bulwark or a rampart, which is a fortification, wall, or embankment built to protect the warriors who shot arrows, threw lances or rocks, or poured boiling water or oil down on the attacking enemy. Therefore, a fortress with built-in ramparts or bulwarks was the ultimate protection for those being attacked.

In several psalms, the Lord is referred to as "my fortress," "my bulwark," or "my rampart." The author of those psalms acknowledged God as his ultimate protection from the weapons of Satan. God is not only our most powerful defense, He's our *only* protection. No earthly weapon or defense system is adequate to safeguard us from the "flaming arrows of the evil one" (Ephesians 6:16).

How do we seek refuge in our Fortress? We must first believe Jesus is Lord and Savior, then worship Him, study His Word, and repent of our sins. And rejoice, knowing His protection is ours!

You are my only protection from Satan, Lord. I'll run to Your shelter and take refuge.

Too Many Options

"Seek the Kingdom of God above all else, and live righteously, and he will give you everything you need."

—Matthew 6:33 NLT

These days, you can easily feel overwhelmed in the cleaning supply aisle of a department store. You'll see dozens of options: gels and sprays and powders, bubbles that scrub, cleaners that are gentle on your floors, others that are ruthless on dirt. But here's a secret many have forgotten: one of the best cleaning solutions by far is water and white vinegar. Fill a bucket with water and add a generous splash of vinegar, and *voila*—you've got a simple but highly effective solution that'll clean everything from windows to hardwood to cabinets.

Sometimes a single day involves far too many options, which makes life far more stressful than joyful. If you can relate, you probably need to come back to the simple "water and vinegar" of effective living: God first, then family, then ministry and career. Don't worry about all those other options until you get your joy and peace back; they'll only confuse you. For right now, focus on the basics that really matter.

Lord, I've been spinning my wheels because there are too many options in an average day. Bring me back to the simple basics of a life well lived.

The Joy of the Race

Let us run with perseverance the race marked out for us.

—Hebrews 12:1

Runners have lots of mottos. Here's a favorite: "I'd rather be the slowest runner in a race any time than a spectator for a lifetime." In other words, watching someone run is no match for the thrill of participating in a race, no matter your pace or fitness level. Similarly, there's a great deal of joy to be had in life even when you're no marathoner, as long as you just keep moving. Sitting on the sidelines, wondering if those Christians might be on to something but too fearful to find out, is not the road to fulfillment.

Here's hope: if you're a born-again believer, you're already in the race. Maybe you started much later than 90 percent of your Christian friends. Maybe you fell down again and again during the first fifteen laps. But you're in the race. You're not a spectator, watching life go by. So just keep moving, with your eyes on the prize: Jesus Himself.

Lord, I'd much rather serve You in the most humble way than to be a mere spectator. Thank You for saving me and allowing me to live this life!

The Joy of Being Known

"I know my sheep and my sheep know me."

—John 10:14

Quick, what's the name of the renowned Leonardo da Vinci painting that features a woman with hands crossed and a demure half-smile?

Did you say *Mona Lisa*? Many folks would say the same, and they'd argue all day long that this is the correct answer. Actually, however, the painting's Italian name is *La Gioconda*. Few people are aware that the portrait features Lisa Gheradini, the wife of a man named Francesco del Giocondo.

How often are we convinced we know the truth about something or someone when we actually know only part of the truth? Maybe you feel that no one knows the real you, even though they think they do. Well, someone *does* know you—the genuine you, the one that perhaps few others have seen. Even better, He *loves* the real you. Living joyfully means understanding that nothing about you is hidden from God. You are fully known, inside and out.

Thank You, Father, that You know me 100 percent, and yet You love me!

Remember Who's in Control

The reality is you have no idea where your life will take you tomorrow.

—James 4:14 VOICE

One mid-December in middle Tennessee, residents of several towns experienced a temperature change of nearly fifty degrees in less than one day. Within twenty-four hours, they saw balmy, springtime weather; tornado warnings; sleet; a dusting of snow; and torrential rain. Not a few commuters left work in short sleeves and arrived home to temperatures in the thirties. Some people were infuriated at the weatherman, others took it in stride, and some found it downright comical.

Life is unpredictable! James 4:14 stresses the importance of always remembering that God is in control, and we are not. In fact, just when we think we know what's going to happen tomorrow, we're running through sleet in nothing but shorts and a T-shirt. It's enough to make a person grumpy, unless we remember that all is well because God knows all about it, and He knows what He's doing. We can trust Him: we might "have no idea where [our] life will take [us] tomorrow," but He's already there.

Lord, help me to take life's randomness in stride. I refuse to forfeit my joy, and I thank You for always being in control.

An Ordinary Life

I sent Tychicus to Ephesus.

—2 Timothy 4:12

There's a misconception in the world that fame and fortune make people extraordinary, and the rest of us, well, we're just the ordinary ones. Do you ever struggle with feeling as if you're living an ordinary life? Tychicus probably would have understood.

Paul's name is mentioned more than one hundred times in Scripture. He served the Lord, loved believers, and suffered greatly, and he did it all well. He was, to put it mildly, extraordinary. No less amazing, however, was Tychicus, who delivered letters from Paul's prison cell to the people in Ephesus. His role of bringing the message was no less important than Paul's role of writing it.

We can begin living joyfully when we understand that ordinary is okay. Whether or not our names are mentioned one hundred times, we're known by the God who created us (Isaiah 43:1). What you do each day matters if you're doing it to the glory of God (1 Corinthians 10:31).

I long to be faithful more than famous, Lord. I'll rejoice knowing that my life is extraordinary if I'm doing Your will.

Joyful Hope

Even if He kills me, I will hope in Him.

—Job 13:15 HCSB

Christ makes a difference in how people grieve. For Christ followers, joy and hope can be ever-present even during tragedy. Scripture doesn't say that we won't grieve, but that we shouldn't grieve like those without hope (1 Thessalonians 4:13).

Job and his wife experienced unspeakable losses and responded differently. Job's wife suggested Job curse God and die (Job 2:9), while Job was determined to cling to God. The same thing that enabled Job to maintain his hope can enable any believer to live joyfully in any situation. Job had an intimate relationship with God long before tragedy struck.

It had always been Job's custom to rise early and pray (Job 1:5). He was completely devoted to God before the heartache and loss. Life is hard and no one makes it through unscathed, but there's joy for the one who's decided to remain faithful to God.

Whatever comes my way, Lord, I'll cling tightly to You. I'll rejoice because of the hope I have in You.

When Life Is Loud

Be silent before the Sovereign LORD, for the day of the LORD is near.
—Zephaniah 1:7

Are you ever desperate to hear from God? Do you feel you could possibly receive a word from Him if your life just wasn't so loud? Life can be so chaotic and overwhelming that it seems to drown out the voice of the Father.

We often rob ourselves of our own joy because we take on responsibilities we were never meant to handle. For instance, we see a verse about being silent and we begin thinking about ways to make our world quieter. We attempt to silence people; we look for ways to accomplish tasks faster so we'll have more downtime. But God doesn't tell us to make our surroundings silent.

God wants *us*, not our environment, to be silent and still. If we'll quiet our spirits, God can speak over any noise that may be going on around us. If we desire the joy that comes from hearing from the Father, we need to work on silencing the only thing we can control—ourselves.

I'll quiet my heart, Father, so I can hear from You. I know You can speak to me even in the midst of a storm.

The Waves Grew Quiet

They rejoiced when the waves grew quiet. Then He guided them to the harbor they longed for.

—Psalm 107:30 HCSB

Every person encounters a stormy season. It's always better to be prepared, but more often than no, the storm sneaks up on us. A job is outsourced, a spouse leaves, or a dream is crushed, and without warning we find ourselves in the midst of a raging sea.

Thankfully, the storm never catches God by surprise, and He's never unprepared. We can rejoice knowing that He's in complete control of His creation and even the waves must obey His voice (Matthew 8:27). There isn't a single storm that doesn't have to become still at His command.

This world seems to be one storm after another. It often seems that *this one* may just be the one that takes us under. We can live joyfully amid life's storms knowing that one day, God will quiet the waves one final time and guide us to the harbor we've longed for.

The greatest joy of my heart, Lord, is knowing You're guiding me to the harbor I long for where the waves are forever stilled.

Eyes on Jesus

Fixing our eyes on Jesus, the pioneer and perfecter of faith.

—Hebrews 12:2

They call it "driving distracted" if you get caught focusing on something other than the road in front of you while behind the wheel. While this kind of distraction is against the law, many of us live distracted every day. One of Satan's greatest tricks is to keep us so busy looking at the latest shiny thing that we lose sight of our Savior.

Whatever captures our attention will hold our gaze. We forget what really matters when we are distracted by worthless things (Psalm 119:37). The world is full of worthless things that will catch our eye and steal our joy. If we take our eyes off Jesus, we will lose sight of God's plan for our life.

God wants you to run the race He has planned for you without distractions. He wants you to keep your eyes fixed on Him so you can persevere, so you will not "grow weary and lose heart" (Hebrews 12:3). The joy waiting for you at the end of the race will keep you going until the race is won.

You're the source of all my joy, Lord. Whatever chaos surrounds me, I'll keep my eyes on You.

Joy in Community

Every day they continued to meet together in the temple courts.
They broke bread in their homes and ate together with glad and
sincere hearts.

—Acts 2:46

ow often do you get together with fellow believers? Do you see them only during worship services or church activities? For some reason, it's common to section off our "church life" from our other interests or activities.

The church people in Acts weren't perfect, but they certainly understood the joy of living in community with other believers. They obeyed the command to regularly worship together (Hebrews 10:25). Many of us also gather on a regular basis to worship, but these believers went even further; they gathered to enjoy meals in each other's homes.

We can have the joy of living in community by following the early church's example. No Pinterest boards or complicated recipes required; the first-century home gatherings were filled with only gladness and simplicity. Let's make it a habit to not only gather to worship, but also to break bread with fellow believers in our homes.

There's such joy in being with fellow believers. Teach me to pause
and break bread with gladness and sincerity.

Better Than I Deserve

I will sing the LORD's praise, for he has been good to me.

How do you view your lot in life? Are you in awe of what God has done with you, through you, and for you? Or did you think at this point you'd have or be more? Many people miss out on joy by failing to recognize the goodness of God in their lives.

David was able to live joyfully because he knew how good the Lord had been to him. He understood the mercy of God and that He doesn't deal with us according to our sins (Psalm 103:10). Instead, in His goodness, He sent His Son to take the wrath we deserved (2 Corinthians 5:21).

There was an old pastor who, when asked how he was, would always respond, "Better than I deserve." If we had the same understanding, we'd be singing joyfully to the Lord every day for all the good He's done.

Thank You, God, for Your goodness to me. When I deserved death, Your Son came and took the wrath for me.

Joy in the Quirks

Imitate God, therefore, in everything you do, because you are his dear children.

—Ephesians 5:1 NLT

Be yourself, they say. But sometimes it's a little scary to own one's true self, the person God designed each of us to be, because that person doesn't fit in as well as the next one. But true joy comes when we dare to be who we're made to be, quirks and all.

Quirky isn't synonymous with *flawed*. "Outside the box" isn't a bad thing. Jesus was very outside the box. So were John the Baptist, Hosea, Deborah, Esther . . . and so on.

As you grow and mature in the Lord, certain interests, strengths, and traits will show themselves, and some of them might be a little unusual. Maybe you've discovered you'd rather serve homeless men and prostitutes than have a more traditional ministry. Or perhaps you love motorcycles and dreadlocks more than sedans and refined haircuts. Maybe you'd rather adopt six kids than bear your own biological children. Good news: you don't have to conform to any particular, idealized Christian image—except for one: Jesus Himself.

Lord, I don't always fit inside the box, but neither did You. Make me more like You every day, no matter what that means!

Dancing Before the Lord

And David danced before the LORD with all his might.

—2 Samuel 6:14 ESV

Have you ever been so filled with joy that you couldn't help but dance? What would it take to bring about that kind of response in you? One thing is for sure: when that level of joy hits you, it won't matter who's watching.

This is the only instance in all of Scripture where this word for dancing (*karar*) is used. The word describes a twirling and whirling type of dance. Can't you see David with his arms outstretched and his head thrown back as he spins with pure joy? What could have caused such a reaction?

The ark of the covenant was coming back to Jerusalem; the presence of God was returning to David's kingdom. What if we got twirly-whirly excited over God's presence in our lives? The presence of God isn't just in our city, but within us! That should cause us to dance with all our might before the Lord.

How amazing, God, that You would choose to dwell within Your people. May I live with joy each day because of Your presence.

Day of Christ

"Your father Abraham rejoiced at the thought of seeing my day; he saw it and was glad."

—John 8:56

What event would you love to witness? A royal wedding, a loved one's return, or a miraculous healing? Everyone has something that causes his or her heart to rejoice at the mere thought of it. For Abraham, that event was the coming of the Messiah.

Jesus told the Jews that Abraham rejoiced at the thought of seeing the coming of Christ. Much the same way, we as believers should rejoice as we anticipate His return. We're told that we'll see Him as He is (1 John 3:2). When John was given his glimpse into heaven, he discovered that the servants of the Lord will see His face (Revelation 22:4).

How can the people of God not live joyfully knowing that we will, one day, gaze upon the face of the Messiah with unveiled eyes? May it be said of us that we rejoiced at the mere thought of seeing that day.

I don't know how it will all play out, Lord, but I'll live joyfully each day, knowing this could be the day I see You face-to-face.

No Longer Sad

"Oh, thank you, sir!" she exclaimed. Then she went back and began to eat again, and she was no longer sad.

—1 Samuel 1:18 NLT

Are you living with the sadness of an unfulfilled desire (1 Samuel 1:5)? You've prayed about it and asked everyone you know to pray as well. You've experienced other things that should have brought joy, but the ache of that one thing continues year after year (1 Samuel 1:7).

Hannah was consumed with grief over her lack of children. She suffered for years until one day she suddenly wiped her tears, began to eat, and was no longer sad. What made such a difference? Eli gave her a blessing, and she believed it would come to pass.

We would begin to live joyfully if we truly believed that the Lord would fulfill His promises to us (Luke 1:45). He has good things planned for us, and anything we lose will be restored either on earth or in heaven (Joel 2:25). When we trust God with our lives, we walk away no longer sad.

God, I can live joyfully even when I don't understand Your ways. I believe You'll fulfill Your promises to me.

Our God Reigns

Let the heavens rejoice, let the earth be glad; let them say among the nations, "The LORD reigns!"

—1 Chronicles 16:31

Do you ever listen to national or world news and feel as if everything is spinning completely out of control? There's anger on the Internet, divisions within families, and war across the globe. No wonder people feel overwhelmed. A lot of the uncertainty comes when we forget that God is still in control of His creation.

It doesn't matter what takes place or what disasters are predicted, God's world is firmly established and nothing can happen without His knowledge (1 Chronicles 16:30). A professor once said, "Has it ever occurred to you that nothing has ever occurred to God?" Nothing scares or surprises the Lord who reigns over all.

Confusion and chaos will never lead to a life of joy. Living joyfully is possible only when we remember that the Lord reigns. Whatever today, tomorrow, or next year may bring, we'll rejoice knowing that God has it all under control.

In a world that seems filled with confusion, Lord, I'll be glad because I know that You're still on Your throne.

Seek Peace

Do all that you can to live in peace with everyone.

—Romans 12:18 NLT

orgiveness is a tricky thing, isn't it? It's also very misunderstood. Are we supposed to forgive someone who isn't sorry? What if we seek forgiveness but the person doesn't extend it to us? Attempting to live at peace with people (and Paul did say *everyone*!) can cause a person to lose a little joy if she doesn't focus on the entire instruction.

Paul says, "Do all that *you can*" (emphasis added). Have you intentionally or unintentionally hurt someone? Then you need to attempt to make peace. Whether or not that person forgives you is between him and God.

Has someone hurt you and you harbor ill feelings toward her? You need to forgive her (Ephesians 4:32). Whether or not that person comes to you and seeks forgiveness is between her and God. Freedom and joy come when we do all we can do to live at peace and leave the rest to God.

If there is someone I need to make peace with, Lord, reveal it to me. I will do my part to live at peace with everyone.

You Have Made Me Glad

*Surely you have granted him unending blessings and made him glad
with the joy of your presence.*

—Psalm 21:6

There was a day when multiple generations of a family would live and die in the same town or general area. This is no longer the case for many people. Families are spread across the country, or in some cases, across the globe. Individuals might go months or years or decades without seeing "their people" face-to-face.

If your family lives in various locations, you know that the love you feel for each other is no less than if you were neighbors. The bond is not weakened by the distance. But a special joy comes when you actually get to be in the presence of your loved ones.

David was referring to himself when he said that the Lord made "him" glad with His presence. Joy often accompanies the presence of God (Psalm 16:11). God doesn't have any long-distance relationships with His people. Each one of us individually is made glad by His presence.

*Lord, You have indeed made me glad with Your presence. Thank
You for choosing to be so near Your people.*

Righteous Ones, Rejoice!

Be glad in the LORD and rejoice, you righteous ones; shout for joy, all you upright in heart.

—Psalm 32:11 HCSB

Shame hinders the joyful life. Secret or unconfessed sin will always cause us to hide from the Lord (Genesis 3:8). Those believers who are glad have learned to confess their sins before the Lord and to rejoice in His forgiveness.

Jesus warned, from the very beginning, that we'd have troubles in this life (John 16:33). Many of our troubles are the result of sin. The moment sin entered the garden, thorns and thistles became a part of our everyday existence (Genesis 3:18). Yet in the midst of sin-induced trials, David called for believers to live glad lives and not guilty ones.

Believers can live with joy, not because we're flawless, but because we're forgiven. When we confess our sins, God is faithful to forgive (1 John 1:9), and our faith is counted as righteousness (Genesis 15:6). Then we may live with joy knowing that we, too, are counted as righteous because of what Jesus has done.

I'll confess my sins and not carry the burden of shame, Lord. I'll shout for joy as one who's been made righteous.

Saving Help

But may all who seek you rejoice and be glad in you; may those who long for your saving help always say, "The LORD is great!"

—Psalm 40:16

Where do you turn when you need help? The answer to that question can make a huge difference in the amount of joy you live with each day. Have you ever looked to the wrong thing or person and been disappointed? The world will offer false sources of security, and many people will trust in the wrong thing (Psalm 20:7) and be forced to live with the consequences.

To live joyfully, we must know where to turn in times of trouble. We must say, with all the certainty of the psalmist, that our help comes from the Lord (Psalm 121:2). We can be glad knowing that when we look to God, the help we long for is on the way. The Lord is great, and our hope is never misplaced in Him.

Whatever the need may be and whatever saving we are seeking, we can rejoice knowing that the Lord is more than able. He's been saving His people from the very beginning, and He isn't stopping now.

I will be glad and seek You in every situation. Lord, I'll live with joy knowing that my help comes from You.

Learning Along the Way

There is profit in all hard work.

—Proverbs 14:23 HCSB

What's the best part of your job?

Some people would immediately answer, "Friday!" or "Payday!" But living joyfully means paying attention to not just your hard-earned paycheck but also what you're learning along the way. The joyful reward of a day's work is not just monetary, it's also the inevitable molding and shaping that's happening to you as a person—changes and improvements in your character or skill set you often don't even notice. For example, even an entry-level job can teach a person a great deal about technology, leadership, problem-solving, communication, and taking responsibility. It can mold someone's character by strengthening his or her capacity for patience. It can bring a timid person out of his shell or teach an argumentative individual about the art of negotiation.

If you have a friend who's also a trusted colleague, ask him or her, "Do you feel I'm a more skilled or knowledgeable person than I was the day I was hired? In what way(s)?" You just might be delighted and surprised at the answer.

I want to get as much joy and knowledge out of my workplace as possible. Help me not to miss a thing, Lord, and thank You for my job.

SEPTEMBER 26

The Sky Is Not Falling!

Do everything without grumbling. . . . Then you will shine among them like stars.

—Philippians 2:14–15

Many of the annoyances that steal our joy in an average day aren't worth the energy we put into them. They have far more power to bring us down than they deserve. For example, we spill coffee on the front of our new shirt and react as though the sky is falling. But coffee stains and a ruined shirt are *not* a disaster.

Sometimes we can gain a right perspective by asking ourselves, *What's the worst that can happen?* In the shirt scenario, the very worst outcome is we'll be out twenty-eight dollars for a blouse and spend a single day with an embarrassing splotch on our clothes. That's an irritation, not a crisis. It certainly isn't the best thing that'll happen all day, but you can bet someone else in your office building has recently had their three-thousand-dollar transmission go out.

The next time you suffer a minor annoyance, stop and take a deep breath before you announce to everyone in the office that you have the worst luck in the world. Never sacrifice your energy or joy for a moment's drama.

Lord, help me to see the minor incidents in my life for what they really are. Thank You for teaching me how to retain my daily joy.

A Child's Joy

"Let the children come to me. Don't stop them! For the Kingdom of Heaven belongs to those who are like these children."

—Matthew 19:14 NLT

There ought to be a National Act-Like-a-Kid Day so that everyone would be periodically reminded what pure, innocent joy looks like. On that day, we'd all be required to spend the afternoon with a child, either our own or one borrowed from a relative or friend. With any luck it would rain on that day, and we could spend a couple of hours jumping in puddles rather than stepping around them. Maybe by the end of the afternoon, we'd realize (or be reminded) that the satisfying *splish splash* of a puddle is more important than spotless clothes; that rain boots are more fun than unblemished, fussy shoes; and that ice cream with sprinkles after an excursion in the rain is more fitting than a sensible meal.

If you need a joy pick-me-up, and if you're blessed enough to have little ones at home (or a young niece, nephew, or neighbor available), set aside at least one afternoon in the next week and spend it with them. By the end of the day, your "happy-meter" will be reset and working properly once again.

Help me to know joy in the way a child knows it, Lord! Thank You for their innocent and beautiful hearts.

The Joy of Togetherness

And let us not neglect our meeting together.

—Hebrews 10:25 NLT

Many bird species seem to love gathering together. Some will collect in the treetops, others on telephone wires, and still others in great flocks that swoop and swirl through the skies.

In Hebrews 10:25, Paul urged us to gather with other Christians regularly. We need other Christians to encourage us, pray for us, share testimonies with us, and just connect with us. It's also important for us to worship together. Although the best way to meet might be in our church buildings, we can even benefit from gathering over a cup of coffee.

Do birds discuss their problems as they perch in the treetops? We don't know. But we do know that Christians need to share with other Christians. This is especially true in difficult times—the very times when people tend to avoid others. The early Christians gathered in homes, ate a meal together, and then prayed and worshipped together. There is great joy in this kind of meeting. Don't neglect it!

Thank You, Lord, for my Christian brothers and sisters. Don't let me neglect meeting with them regularly.

The Aroma and Flavor of Jesus

For we are to God the pleasing aroma of Christ.

—2 Corinthians 2:15

hat's your favorite meal? Spinach lasagna? Lobster bisque? Barbecued ribs? Some of the best dishes include an ingredient or two that are obvious and concentrated, such as horseradish on a steak. But others make our mouths water by taking a more subtle approach: for example, if you add a bay leaf to a pot of chicken and dumplings and then allow the pot to gently simmer, the flavor of the leaf will permeate everything, from the chicken to the dumplings themselves. This subtle flavor holds everything else together, so to speak, and the gentle aroma will permeate every single bite.

In the life of a Christian, joy is like that bay leaf: it's not always obvious, but it flavors everything we do and say. If you carry the joy of the Lord, others might not always be able to put their finger on what's different about you, but they'll pick up on the fragrance and flavor of Jesus in your words, attitude, and actions.

Starting right now, in every circumstance and situation, I want to be flavored with the joy that only You can give me, Jesus.

A Harvest of Joy

Those who sow in tears will reap with shouts of joy.

—Psalm 126:5 HCSB

If we were to focus only on the here and now, we'd live lives of sorrow with intermittent glimpses of joy. If the harvest were dependent on only our efforts, it would hardly be worth the sweat and tears. Praise Jesus that He's the Lord of the harvest (Matthew 9:38).

At some point, everyone will enter a season where all he seems to sow are tears. Death, divorce, and division can seem unredeemable. Yet we have the promise of a bountiful harvest with Christ. Our tears don't go unnoticed by our heavenly Father (Psalm 56:8); they water the ground, which in due time will produce sprouts of joy.

We must keep plowing and planting with patience, knowing it'll be worth it if we don't give up (Galatians 6:9). There can be joy in each day, in the midst of each pain, when we live with the harvest in mind.

Lord, give me the endurance and patience I need to sow seeds of faith so that at the proper time, I'll reap a harvest of joy.

OCTOBER

Rejoicing Before God

But the righteous are glad; they rejoice before God and celebrate with joy.

—Psalm 68:3 HCSB

How do you feel when you're in the presence of someone you've wronged? You probably feel a little guilty or embarrassed; maybe you feel angry with the other person. You may attempt to avoid her altogether for fear she'll seek revenge or even demand that you leave her presence.

According to David, this is how the wicked feel when in the presence of God. They'll either flee or be scattered (Psalm 68:1). Either way, the wicked or unrepentant will not be allowed to enjoy the blessings of standing before Him.

The righteous, however, are glad when in the Lord's presence. They rejoice and celebrate before Him because they've known the beauty of being set free through the blood of Christ. They can stand before Him forgiven and unashamed. Those who have trusted in God's Son can celebrate with joy knowing they're welcome in His sight.

There's no place I'd rather be, Lord, than in Your presence. Because of what Jesus has done, I can rejoice before You.

OCTOBER 2

The Yoke and Burden of Jesus

"My yoke is easy to bear, and the burden I give you is light."
—Matthew 11:30 NLT

Your three-year-old wants to help you with a weekend project, so you say, "Great! Help me carry this two-by-four to the garage." As the two of you make your way across the backyard, he's clueless that you're shouldering 99.8 percent of the weight while you let him think he's doing all the work. That way he'll learn to pitch in when others need help, and he'll feel the joy and sense of accomplishment that come from teaming up with Mom or Dad to get the job done.

As Christians, we're commanded to carry a yoke, but too often we try to shoulder a million burdens that aren't ours to carry—and then wonder why we implode under the stress. We've been instructed to carry Jesus' yoke and burden, not our own. Our shoulders can handle only so much, but His are infinitely strong.

Jesus carries the brunt of the load, allowing us to bend but not break, and keeping His eye on us the whole time. What a joy to be loved by such a good God!

Lord Jesus, help me to throw off everything I'm not meant to carry and instead take Your yoke and burden.

Unfailing Love

*Satisfy us in the morning with your unfailing love, that we may sing
for joy and be glad all our days.*

—Psalm 90:14

ow good does it feel to be loved? Romance authors attempt to put it into words, and songwriters try to give it a melody. The Beatles were convinced that at the end of the day, love is all you need; the psalmist would agree that genuine love is synonymous with God's love.

If we could truly grasp how much God loves us (Ephesians 3:18), we would sing for joy and be glad all of our days. Every morning when we arise, we can know that we're loved; His love is unfailing and His mercies are brand new (Lamentations 3:23).

God's love is greater than any trial we face, any mistake we make, or any betrayal we endure. When the enemy attempts to plant seeds of doubt, believers can rejoice knowing they're loved by the God who is the embodiment of love (1 John 4:8).

*Lord, Your relationship with Your people is the greatest love story
ever told. May I always rejoice because of that love.*

Looking Back with Gratitude

For you make me glad by your deeds, LORD; I sing for joy at what your hands have done.

—Psalm 92:4

Whether a parent, spouse, or friend, we are all guilty of taking someone we care about for granted from time to time. However, if we would take the time to list all of the ways people have blessed us, we'd be filled with gratitude and joy. Looking back, we'd probably recognize gifts that we didn't appreciate in the moment.

Think of the things the Lord has done for you (Psalm 9:1). There are times when He's provided for financial needs, granted healing, or blessed you through the people He placed in your path. He's given peace in the midst of chaos and comfort in times of pain. He's given you grace to go on when you thought you were at the end of your rope.

Anytime you begin to feel cold toward the Lord, begin recounting His deeds (Isaiah 63:7), and you'll be made glad. You'll see His hand in a variety of circumstances, and you'll sing for joy.

I'm aware, Lord, of Your glorious deeds. Thank You for working wonders among Your people.

Gladness of Heart

They seldom reflect on the days of their life, because God keeps them occupied with gladness of heart.

—Ecclesiastes 5:20

Do you ever find yourself considering the brevity of life? This usually happens when someone we love is ill or we experience an unexpected loss. We all know that we're not promised tomorrow (Proverbs 27:1), but certain experiences may cause us to dwell on this fact a little longer than usual. This isn't the way God intends for us to live.

According to Solomon, believers are able to live joyfully when they're not consumed with the sorrows or brevity of life. They see all activities as gifts from God; they rejoice whether eating and drinking or toiling under the sun (Ecclesiastes 5:18). They don't look back and spend time pondering all of the "what ifs" of life.

To live joyfully is to focus on today (Psalm 118:24) and to be filled with the gladness that each day offers. There's work to be done and joy to be experienced right now. Let's be occupied with that.

Lord, focusing on an uncertain tomorrow brings sadness. Thank You for the joy You've placed in my heart for the things of today.

Trusting Him

*In that day they will say, "Surely this is our God; we trusted in him,
and he saved us. This is the LORD, we trusted in him; let us rejoice
and be glad in his salvation."*

—Isaiah 25:9

What's your first reaction when someone says, "Trust me"? "Famous last words"? "I've heard that before"? "Yeah, right"?

Many of us have been let down one too many times, and trust doesn't always come easily. But, if we're fortunate, we also have a person in our lives whose word is good.

One day, we'll never again experience disappointment. Isaiah describes a time when God will swallow death forever and will wipe away the tears. In that day, believers will say, "We trusted Him. We trusted Him when times were difficult. We trusted Him when people walked away. We trusted Him when pain came our way."

We can live with joy because on that day we'll know our trust was always well placed. We trusted Him and He saved us. We trusted Him, we received the salvation He promised, and we'll be eternally glad.

*Lord, when the end comes and I stand face-to-face with You in
glory, I'll be glad to say, "I trusted You all along."*

Grace of God

When he arrived and saw what the grace of God had done, he was glad and encouraged them all to remain true to the Lord with all their hearts.

—Acts 11:23

How glad are you when you see the grace of God in someone's life? If you've ever prayed fervently for someone to come to the Lord and it happened, then you know gladness. Or perhaps you've witnessed a fellow believer walk through a terrible trial and remain faithful. That, too, is due to the grace of God in a person's life.

When Stephen was stoned to death (Acts 7:54–60), Christ followers scattered due to persecution, but many were spreading the good news to Greeks as well as Jews. Barnabas traveled to Antioch to check on the believers there and found that, through the grace of God, the church was growing. Barnabas was glad and stayed to encourage them (Acts 11:19–24).

Witnessing the grace of God is certainly a joyful experience, and it's happening all around us. If we wish to add some joy to our lives, let's ask God to allow us to witness Him at work and to be a source of encouragement to fellow believers.

Lord, allow me to see Your grace in the lives of others. Let me inspire joy in my fellow believers.

Salvation for All

And when the Gentiles heard this, they began rejoicing and glorifying the word of the Lord, and as many as were appointed to eternal life believed.

—Acts 13:48 ESV

Imagine the greatest gift in the world being offered to people around you—but not to you. How would that make you feel? Then imagine the giver of the gift saying that it was now available to everyone (Acts 13:47).

The Gentiles were filled with joy when they were told that the gift of salvation was for Jews and Gentiles alike. The greatest gift of all was now for them, too, and the magnitude of it wasn't lost on them. How often do you rejoice because you've been offered the precious gift of salvation?

We would live with joy daily if we fully grasped the awesomeness of the gift offered to us. Only the grace of God makes such amazing salvation possible for any who would believe (Titus 2:11). We don't have to be of a certain social standing and education level to receive the gift. This news should make us rejoice!

Thank You, Lord, that Your salvation is for all people. I'll live with joy because I'm a recipient of that gift.

Share in Suffering

That I may know him and the power of his resurrection, and may share his sufferings, becoming like him in his death.

—Philippians 3:10 ESV

The world tends to equate a lack of suffering with the favor of God. Someone makes it through life somewhat unscathed, hashtags it all *#blessed*, and foolishly believes it's a sign of God's love. Paul would have a very different view of the *#blessed* life.

In his letter to the Philippians, Paul stated that everything he did was so that he would know Christ, know the power of His resurrection, and "share his sufferings." Paul counted it a privilege and a joy to suffer for Christ (Colossians 1:24).

We can begin to live joyfully when we stop seeing every instance of suffering as punishment from God. Every hardship and heartache is a chance to be more like Christ. Every trial becomes an opportunity to walk as He walked (1 John 2:6). Then, looking back, we'll realize that we lived quite a *#blessed* life.

I will rejoice in suffering, Lord, if it works to conform me to the image of Christ. I'll count it all joy as Paul did.

God Sends People

I rejoiced in the Lord greatly that now at length you have revived your concern for me. You were indeed concerned for me, but you had no opportunity.

—Philippians 4:10 ESV

f you've ever had someone sit next to your hospital bed, stand beside you at a graveside, or serve you during a time of need, then you're intimately acquainted with one of God's greatest gifts. There's something immensely comforting about knowing someone is concerned about us. God, in His love for us, never intended for us to navigate life alone.

The truth is that Christ is always enough. There may be times when He's all you have, and in those moments you'll discover that your Savior is more than sufficient (Philippians 4:13). Yet there are other times when He so graciously places people in our lives who are able to empathize (Philippians 4:14).

We can live joyfully knowing that just when we need it, God will place a fellow sojourner in our path. In the meantime, we can also find joy by comforting others in their time of need.

Thank You, Lord, for the people You've placed in my life. There's joy in the comfort of a friend who cares.

The God Who Provides

And my God will meet all your needs according to the riches of his glory in Christ Jesus.

—Philippians 4:19

Sometimes we buy into the lie that we've got to have the biggest, brightest, most expensive "toys." Our eyes never tire of seeing, and our bellies never get their fill (Ecclesiastes 1:8). Our list of needs seems endless, and we worry about not having enough.

If asked, you could probably list a number of things you're currently concerned about. Perhaps there are needs you aren't certain will be met. But what if we didn't worry about every little thing? What if we trusted God to do what He's promised to do: supply every single need? Truth be told, He knows what our needs are better than we do anyway (Matthew 6:8).

No one and nothing in this world can meet our every need. But when we walk with God, we'll "lack nothing" (Psalm 23:1). We can live joyfully knowing that the One who created us knows how to care for us.

God, You know what I need in every season. I can live joyfully knowing that You'll always take care of me.

Prayer and Praise

Are any of you suffering hardships? You should pray. Are any of you happy? You should sing praises.

—James 5:13 NLT

There are two responses to every situation a believer may face. If you're going through a trying time, James's instruction is to pray. If things are going well for you at the moment, songs of praise should be on your lips.

The beautiful thing about the life of a believer is that he or she can experience equal joy in both times of prayer and times of praise. During times of suffering, we can trust the One who hears our prayers; during times of praise, we can thank the One from whom all good things come (James 1:17). There's joy in both because there's Jesus in both.

A believer's life can be filled with joy because Scripture gives instructions on how to navigate every season and situation. The Word applies perfectly to whatever we're going through, and we have joy and Jesus whether we're praying or praising.

I have access to You, Lord, in every season of life. Whether I'm enduring hardship or experiencing happiness, I will rejoice.

The Joy of Learning

Let the wise listen and add to their learning.

—Proverbs 1:5

Imagine a couple whose kids have all moved away. To keep themselves from slipping into a rut, the husband signs up for a class at the local college, and the wife begins walking every morning with a friend. Is one choice better than the other?

In our society, which places great emphasis on physical fitness, we might be tempted to say that the wife has made the better choice (and indeed she's made a good one). But we mustn't overlook the fact that people who experience joy in life are often those who never stop learning. There's activity (not to be confused with busyness), and then there's learning. Ask yourself: *Am I still learning, or did that stop the moment I finished my final college class? Do I apply myself to gaining new knowledge several times a week?* If not, find a way to expand your mind. Learn a new language. Memorize Psalm 91. Read a collection of poetry until you find a style you love. Never lose the joy of learning!

Lord, is there something You'd like me to learn at this stage in my life? Tell me what it is, and help me to always keep learning.

True Relationship

One who has unreliable friends soon comes to ruin, but there is a friend who sticks closer than a brother.

—Proverbs 18:24

Every human being longs for intimacy. We all yearn to connect first with our Creator, and then each other. When that doesn't happen, we might look to society, which offers a thousand and one ways to temporarily and inadequately fill the need for connection via the Internet. Online, we can instantly join groups, carry on long conversations with people all over the globe who share our interests, or even find a romantic interest—without ever interacting face-to-face with a human being. These connections aren't always negative, but if we start to believe they offer all we need regarding intimacy, we'll lose all joy, and we'll feel empty.

True relationship can be found only in and through God, our Maker. Doesn't it make sense that the One who made us knows exactly how to fulfill and connect with us?

There's nothing inherently wrong with technology or even social media, but be cautious: Are you spending more time on virtual relationships than on real ones? If so, commit to turning your attention back to the joy of genuine relationships.

Thank You for the tool of social media, but help me to never replace real friendships with virtual ones, Lord.

Passing on Knowledge

"The student who is fully trained will become like the teacher."
—Luke 6:40 NLT

One of the surest ways to experience joy in your work is to pass on the knowledge you've gained to the next generation. But how can you know who is and isn't a worthwhile investment? After all, not everyone has the potential or desire to move forward and learn from his or her superiors.

Here are a few things to look for in a future leader:

Goal-oriented: he or she sets both short- and long-term goals for him- or herself.

Proactive: a future leader will be willing to do more than the minimum job requirements.

Creative: he or she will find a creative solution to a problem rather than giving up or passing the task on to someone else.

Inquisitive: in the quest for knowledge, a trailblazer asks questions and always wants to know who, why, and how.

Take a look around your workplace and find an eager young man or woman who fits the bill; then invest in that person's life and watch your own job satisfaction increase by leaps and bounds.

Would You like me to pass on some of the things You've allowed me to learn in my workplace, Lord? Please show me whom I'm to mentor.

OCTOBER 16

God, My Security

It is God who arms me with strength and keeps my way secure.
—Psalm 18:32

You're alone in the house, standing on a stepstool, trying to reach the top shelf of your tall, heavy bookcase, when your foot slips; you grab hold of the bookcase as you topple backward, the bookcase on top of you. You know you're hurt, but you can't reach your phone. With no one else around to help you, you cry out to God, "Lord, help me!"

The next day the newspaper carries the story of how you managed to lift a heavy bookcase off your legs, slide yourself to your phone, and call an ambulance. Where did that strength come from? Naturally, the paper talks about "a surge of adrenaline" that enabled you to perform the Herculean lift, but you know better: you cried out to God, and He answered.

The world has a "logical" explanation for stories like these, but God's children know better. We have every reason to sing to the Lord with joy. Again and again, our almighty God proves that He is our Strength, and our security is in Him!

My heart soars with joy, Lord, when I think of how often You've provided what I've needed. Thank You for being my Strength, my Provider, and my Security.

Seek the Lord's Counsel

Then the men of Israel took some of their provisions, but did not seek the LORD's counsel.

—Joshua 9:14 HCSB

Have you ever had a great idea, gone full steam ahead with it, and fallen flat on your face? You're not alone. A certain young woman had five small children and a couple of part-time jobs, but she thought it would be a great idea to lead an early morning Bible study at church. Let's just say that no one in that class looked at her and thought, "Look at that joyful woman."

Looking back, she was embarrassed to realize she hadn't sought the Lord's counsel on whether or not to lead that class. It turned out to be an extremely stressful six weeks. That's what happens when we plan things without asking for God's input. If the Lord isn't in it, it will not bring us any joy, and we may even fail miserably.

We can save ourselves a lot of stress if we learn to ask for the Lord's guidance before we make decisions. Whether it's a potential spouse, a career change, or an overload of responsibilities, let's take a moment and seek the Lord's counsel. When we know He is behind it, we can joyfully take on any challenge.

I don't want to take a single step, Lord, without seeking Your counsel. I long for the joy that comes only from being in Your will.

The Road to Emmaus

We had hoped he was the Messiah who had come to rescue Israel.
This all happened three days ago.

—Luke 24:21 NLT

A re you ever overwhelmed by the "ugly" that seems to permeate this world? We might be tempted to stay inside our homes, close the blinds, watch *Little House on the Prairie* reruns, and wait for Jesus to come back. There are times when we've stormed the gates of heaven with prayers, and the outcome was still not as we hoped.

Picture the men on the road to Emmaus. They were men who had believed but didn't fully understand. The Teacher whom they'd joyfully followed was dead, and though they heard rumors of the resurrection, they just weren't sure. Then Jesus arrived and brought the joy of revelation with Him (Luke 24:27).

Sometimes we don't understand what has taken place, and we may be tempted toward discouragement. Let's choose joy instead, knowing that one day everything will be revealed, our eyes will be opened, and we'll see clearly (1 Corinthians 13:12).

When the world seems too much, Lord, I'll trust in the joy that one day will be mine when You reveal Yourself once more.

No More Hiding

*Then the woman, knowing what had happened to her, came and
fell at his feet and, trembling with fear, told him the whole truth.*

—Mark 5:33

What stands between you and true joy in Christ? Apart
from sin, the biggest barrier we encounter is shame.
That's why we often want our healing to happen in private.
We believe in His power, but our instinct is to touch the
hem of His robe and then disappear into the crowd (Mark
5:28).

Jesus is interested in more than simply healing our
hurts; He wants to draw us out of hiding so we may know
His joy. The woman in Mark 5 had already been physically
healed, but He was insistent upon seeing her face to face
(Mark 5:32). She came in shame, but He wanted her to
leave in joy.

Satan wants you to hide in the dark with your shame,
but Jesus says, "Come" (Matthew 11:28). He can heal from
afar (John 4:53), but joy happens in His presence. Let's
come out of hiding and share in the Master's joy (Matthew
25:23).

*No more hiding, Lord. I'm choosing to let go of my shame so that I
can take hold of Your joy.*

God of Compassion

"I have compassion for these people; they have already been with me three days and have nothing to eat."

—Mark 8:2

Have you ever stepped out in faith and followed Jesus? Did you end up in a place where you wouldn't survive if He didn't provide? There's joy knowing that God has compassion on His people.

A multitude of people followed Jesus' earthly ministry. They had left the comfort of their homes and all they had in order to follow Jesus; they didn't want to miss a single lesson He taught. They were so intent on following Him that they didn't even stop to pack food. The disciples might have sent them away, but Jesus had compassion because He knew how far they'd traveled (Mark 8:3).

We can follow God with joy knowing that He's fully aware what it costs us to follow, and He has compassion (Romans 9:18). We can serve Him faithfully, trusting that God will "have compassion on His servants" (Psalm 135:14).

I will follow You with Joy, Jesus, trusting in Your compassion to care for my needs when other people would send me away.

Meditate

Instead, his delight is in the LORD's instruction, and he meditates on it day and night.

—Psalm 1:2 HCSB

Do you ever feel you read God's Word but you miss the delight? You read the words, but they don't seem to stick with you as you go throughout the day. Many times we miss out on the joy of the Lord's instruction because we read but we don't meditate.

The psalmist said that the person who delights in the reading of God's Word *and* meditates on it day and night is blessed. To live joyfully, we must take what He's taught us and meditate on it during our days and into the night.

If we delight in His Word, God will bring appropriate truths to our minds when we encounter troubles or disappointments in our day-to-day walk. This is just one benefit of focusing and meditating on the things of God. When we begin to feel burdened, we will look up and wait expectantly for Him (Psalm 5:3).

Thank You, God, for the joy that Your Word brings. I will delight in Your instruction and continually meditate upon it.

Prone to Wander

I have strayed like a lost sheep. Seek your servant, for I have not forgotten your commands.

—Psalm 119:176

Have you ever felt you were prone to wander? You're on fire for the Lord, and then you're not. One minute you're loving toward others, and the next you're not. It happens to all of us, so how can we maintain joy in a season of drifting?

First, we stay put and let the Lord seek us. Like a child lost in a store, we are wise if we simply stay still. Sometimes we don't know exactly what caused us to wander away. Sometimes we're not sure if we've wandered away or if we're just really tired. There comes a point when we just need to stop, be still, and wait for the Lord to give us direction.

Second, we must stay in the Word even when we feel a bit lost. This is how we're going to recognize the sound of the Lord's voice. Many people and things are vying for our attention, and we need to know His voice.

Finally, we can't be ashamed to call for help. Being still does not *always* mean being silent.

When I know I'm not where I should be, I'll call out to You, Lord, and listen for the sound of Your voice.

Joy in Your Work

Whatever your hand finds to do, do it with all your might.

—Ecclesiastes 9:10

College professors are well aware that older students ("nontraditional" students, they're sometimes called) are attentive and studious learners. They have enough experience under their belts to appreciate how much their education is costing, so they tend to take their studies very seriously and often make good grades. Because they're past the days when staying up all night on the weekends was fun, they're more diligent and attentive, with fewer missed classes. Most will tell you that making a change later in life isn't easy . . . but it *is* entirely possible and incredibly rewarding. Whatever you decide to do, do it with your whole heart.

Few things are greater than taking joy in your career, so if yours is no longer fulfilling, maybe it's time to continue your education. Yes, you might have to do a lot of juggling, and your friends might think you've lost your marbles, and it's an unusual thing to do. But *unusual* does not equal *impossible*.

Lord, do I need to make room for change by taking some classes? Please give me direction and confidence to do what You're calling me to do.

Our All-or-Nothing God

Despite all your many offenses, He forgives and releases you.
—Psalm 103:3 VOICE

ave you ever met someone with an all-or-nothing per-sonality? You ask them to turn the air conditioner up a little and they flip the switch to *ten*, never noticing the frost forming on the windows. They find out the new neighbors—a family of four—are coming over for dinner, and they cook enough for thirty. They don't seem to know how to do anything halfway.

Jesus has an all-or-nothing attitude when it comes to forgiveness. In *What You Need to Know About Salvation*, Max Anders says, "Jesus pays for all our sin or none of it." In other words, we have no business accepting forgiveness for certain sins while hanging on to the guilt and shame of others. Yet many of us have "that one sin" that still plagues us.

Maybe you need to make an all-or-nothing decision regarding your past: either take back the guilt of every sin you've ever committed, or let Jesus take the guilt and punishment of *every single one*. Stop holding on to something that, in the mind of God, doesn't even exist. Be free and full of joy!

Lord, I want to be free. I confess right now that You paid for all my sin, and I will be eternally grateful!

The Unalterable Truth

"I am the Living One."

—Revelation 1:18

Through a combination of just the right temperature, moisture, and wind, lenticular clouds take on a saucer shape and sometimes look much like UFOs. If the setting sun hits them just right, the result can be quite convincing. More than one person has frantically snapped photos and alerted the media that aliens were about to land. But all the while, the "UFO" was just a cloud. No matter how fervently the "witness" insisted that the little green men had arrived, the cloud never became a flying saucer. Why not? Because believing a thing to be true doesn't make it true.

Sometimes we Christians forget this. We're surrounded by unbelievers who insist that our beliefs are fairy tales, that God is dead, that truth is relative, and that there's no such thing as moral absolutes. But remember: even if every person on earth were to insist that your God was a figment of your imagination, God wouldn't cease to be God. Rejoice! His existence, and His love for you, are completely unaffected by the naysayers in your life.

Bless the people in my life who have rejected You, Lord, and thank You that You're more real than the air I'm breathing.

Avoiding Materialism

Those who want to get rich fall into temptation and a trap.
—1 Timothy 6:9

Persian vipers were discovered only about ten years ago. Their "claim to fame" is their tail, which looks like a large, grotesque spider. When an unsuspecting little animal approaches the "spider," hoping for a snack, it instead *becomes* the snack when it's devoured by the viper. The "spider" isn't a spider at all; it's a method of distracting the animal and bringing it within the viper's reach.

Think of materialism as the distraction that will veer you off the joyful course that God has planned for you and into the mouth of the enemy. Materialism has turned more than a few joyful believers into fearful or greedy human beings. The moment they were "swallowed up" by the need for more, their testimony of grace and gratitude was rendered ineffective. This isn't to say that we're in danger of being duped by the enemy every time we think, *Gee, I'd like to have that*—but that a Christian's joy and fulfillment come only from the heart of Jesus.

If I've given in to materialism in even the smallest way, Lord, please show me. Put me back on the path to real joy and fulfillment in You.

God Knows

You are the God who sees me.

—Genesis 16:13

Quick: What's the most abundant element in our planet's atmosphere? If you're like most people who don't think much about chemistry, you probably answered, "Oxygen." But there's actually more than three times the nitrogen in the air around you right now than oxygen. Even so, most of us rarely think or talk about nitrogen or acknowledge its importance—even though we'd be in big trouble without it.

Does your family sometimes fail to acknowledge the effort and time you put into bringing home the bacon, keeping the finances in order, doing the bulk of the household chores, or making sure the kids are fed, clothed, and cared for in a thousand other ways? Have you ever thought, *They'd be in a fix if I weren't around!* Then consider this: the fact that no one discusses nitrogen doesn't lessen its importance one iota. Find joy in the fact that even as you're changing what feels like your millionth stinky diaper, God sees. God knows. Your role is crucial, and your diligence pleases Him.

Lord, I choose joy simply because You see—and are pleased with— all that I do for my family, and that's enough.

Gleaning from the Joy

A person can do nothing better than to eat and drink and find satisfaction in their own toil. This too, I see, is from the hand of God.

—Ecclesiastes 2:24

Most of us would agree that people can learn valuable lessons from the things they've suffered. But sometimes we forget that we can glean much from our experiences whether they're negative *or* positive. That's right, an easy, pleasant season isn't just a "free pass." When we're tuned in to the Holy Spirit, we can learn oodles from our mistakes and sorrows but also from the joyful, agreeable experiences that happen at work, at home, and in our relationships. And afterward we often have much to offer others.

Think of a major positive event in your life. Maybe you're a successful artist or author. Perhaps you've enjoyed a decades-long, fulfilling marriage with your high school sweetheart. You were presented with a thousand opportunities to grow, learn, and change even through the wonderful experiences.

Excavate every nugget of truth and growth out of the hard times, but don't forget that the joyful times are gold mines as well.

I'm so grateful, Lord, for the joyful times in my life that have made me a better person by conforming me to Your image.

A Right Perception

Be made new in the attitude of your minds.

—Ephesians 4:23

One of the most simple but vital tools in any kitchen is a colander. Pour a steaming pot of spaghetti through a colander, and the water filters right through the holes, trapping the noodles in the colander. Quick and easy.

Unfortunately, some of us have internal "colanders" that trap the negative and allow the positive to slip right down the drain—along with every bit of joy we might have had. Our boss sits down with us for our annual evaluation, and five minutes later we've forgotten every bit of praise and every compliment; all we can remember is the one piece of constructive criticism. Or we get a *B* on a difficult test, and instead of rejoicing in a good grade, we obsess about the few questions we missed.

Living joyfully requires the ability to perceive what others are saying without ignoring *or* magnifying the things we don't especially want to hear. If your mind tends to "trap" all that's negative and forget all that's positive, ask the Lord to mend your perception.

Help me examine the way I perceive the good versus the bad, Lord, and help me make adjustments as needed so that I don't forfeit my joy.

The Joy of Being Ransomed

"The Son of Man did not come to be served, but to serve, and to give his life as a ransom for many."

—Matthew 20:28

Several blockbuster movies that have kept us on the edge of our seats have involved the concept of ransom: a child or spouse is kidnapped, and the parent or partner stops at nothing to rescue the captive. We love these movies because they're exciting, and we shout for joy when the loved one is ransomed and saved from harm in the nick of time.

Ancient societies were familiar with the concept of ransom; this is why we see the word more than a dozen times in the Bible. We can read about the ransom of land in Jeremiah (32:6–15) or of someone guilty of manslaughter in Exodus (21:29–30). People regularly ransomed their relatives who were prisoners of war or who'd sold themselves into slavery to pay a debt.

In the verse above, Jesus declared that He'd soon pay the ransom to free sinners. We couldn't ransom ourselves. The price was far too high. Only Jesus could pay the price, and praise Him, that's what He did. We are the joyful ransomed ones!

Lord, I acknowledge that Satan held me captive until You ransomed me. Thank You!

What About Him?

Peter asked Jesus, "What about him, Lord?"

—John 21:21 NLT

Your preteen daughter's first sleepover is two days away. You encourage her to complete her homework early so she's free to enjoy herself. "But what about *her*?" she whines, pointing at her little sister. "Why doesn't *she* have to finish her homework too?" You swallow your frustration and answer, "Your sister is not involved. Besides, I'm asking you to do this so you can enjoy a party!"

When Jesus said to Peter, "Follow me!" (John 21:19), Peter turned toward John and said, "Lord, what about him?" (v. 21). Peter had to turn briefly to see John (v. 20). When we fret about someone else's calling, we inadvertently turn our eyes away from Jesus and forfeit our joy. We can also open ourselves up to anxiety (if it seems we're not doing enough in comparison), pride (if we feel we're doing a better job than most), or resentment (if we suspect we're doing more than our fair share).

What God does or doesn't do in someone else's life has no bearing on your calling. Resist comparison and choose joy!

Lord, I choose joy and refuse to compare myself or my Christian walk with what You're doing in my brothers' and sisters' lives.

NOVEMBER

Created with Love

*"I knew you before I formed you in your mother's womb.
Before you were born I set you apart and appointed you as
my prophet to the nations."*

—Jeremiah 1:5 NLT

If you've spent much time reading Scripture, there's a pretty good chance you could quote a couple verses off the top of your head. One danger of well-known passages is that we know them by memory but not by heart. We know the words but have lost the wonder.

If we could fully grasp how much thought God put into our very existence, we'd walk with joy each and every day. He shaped us; He knit us together with loving hands, taking every aspect of our bodies and personalities into consideration. He took the time to know us before He ever formed us, and He's deeply concerned with every detail of our lives.

No one is an accident in God's family. He thought of us, physically created us, and has a specific, holy plan for our lives. All people who exist can rejoice knowing that God created him or her in love and on purpose.

*It brings me great joy to know that You looked into time and desired
to create me, Lord. Thank You for the love with which I was made.*

True Joy

In their fright the women bowed down with their faces to the ground, but the men said to them, "Why do you look for the living among the dead?"

—Luke 24:5

Why are we so often shocked when we encounter hardship in this world? Shouldn't we already be aware that the paths are rocky and the terrain is sin-stained? Worldly pursuits will leave us empty, and people inevitably will let us down. Yet we continue to seek joy where none is to be found (Ecclesiastes 2:25).

Picture the women crying at the tomb and the angels asking, "Why do you look for the living among the dead?" Don't we often seek the right things in the wrong places? We try to find joy through our peers, occupations, or accomplishments. If any of these things don't work out the way we would like, we allow our joy to slip away.

We spend too much time searching for the joy of the living Savior among the dead things of the world. The psalmist declared that he relied on the Lord for his well-being (Psalm 16:2). He was aware of the fickleness of joy gained through worldly praise and accomplishments. We'll live joyfully when we seek joy in the correct places.

Lord, I've looked for Your joy in the things of the world. I've learned that everything I need is found in You.

Used by God

And David was the father of Solomon by the wife of Uriah.

—Matthew 1:6 ESV

Have you ever looked at your life and wondered how God could bring anything good out of it? Have you ever looked at your past and thought it would be best buried and forgotten? Maybe you thought your failings and mistakes eliminated you from any joy God may have had planned for you.

When outlining the lineage of Christ, Matthew refers to David's child with "the wife of Uriah." Those words are intended to remind us of the sins of David: his acts of adultery and murder. All too often we think our sins render us useless in the kingdom. Or, once forgiven, we think our sins should be swept under the rug and never mentioned again.

There were twenty-eight generations between David and Christ—between a sinful, broken wretch of a man and the holy, sinless Savior of the world (Matthew 1:17). Joy and beauty were still to come for David, and there are for each of us as well.

Praise You, Lord, for the beauty of forgiveness and the gift of joy that are mine through confession and repentance.

Surviving Good-Bye

There is nothing on earth that I desire besides you.

—Psalm 73:25 ESV

How many times have you had to say good-bye? No matter how much we wish it were different, good-bye is a part of life. Circumstances change, people change, and good-byes are painful. We often must leave a situation or relationship that we hold dear. Sometimes we have no say in the matter; we lose someone to an illness or tragedy. No matter the scenario, good-byes are rarely good.

Through it all, we learn to hold very loosely to the things of this world. We hold the things and people we cherish in open palms and not closed fists. We entrust those we love to God, knowing that He loves them even more. We choose to live joyfully knowing that He can redeem any loss.

The key to maintaining joy in the midst of good-bye is to desire God more than anything this world has to offer. It's okay to grieve what we've lost. The joy comes when we can look at the loss and still say, "Lord, You are enough."

Good-byes are painful, and I don't like them, Lord, but I can say with joy that You're all I need.

Finding Joy

Rejoice in the Lord always. I will say it again: Rejoice!

—Philippians 4:4

Paul instructs us to *always rejoice.* We look around at this broken world and wonder how he could expect it of us. Didn't he know that disappointments wait around every bend? That people let each other down? That sickness and death mock us? Haven't we all been there? We read that joy will come in the morning, but we aren't sure how to make it through the night.

Paul knew that the world weighs heavy on mortal shoulders and that heaven seems a little too far away some days. He was aware of painful good-byes and wayward children and ill parents. The earth spins fast and anxiety grips us and decisions must be made.

"Rejoice in the Lord," Paul said. It may seem as though he didn't have a clue, but he did understand hardship. He knew that if we leaned on anything except Christ, we'd surely fall. Paul was right in telling us to rejoice in the Lord; there's no joy to be found anywhere else.

I will rejoice, Lord, when times are good, and I'll rejoice when they aren't because in both cases, I always have You.

Inheritance

Surely I have a delightful inheritance.

—Psalm 16:6

What kind of inheritance are you expecting? Perhaps you've already claimed your mama's cookbooks, Grandpa's fishing gear, or Grandma's crocheted blankets. Maybe you don't have any idea what, if anything, you'll receive. Unlike some movie characters, few of us have a mysterious rich relative who passes away and chooses to bestow wealth upon us.

As Christ-followers, we're promised not just any inheritance, but a beautiful one: Christ Himself. His very presence is promised to us, and in His presence we can find fullness of joy and eternal pleasure (Psalm 16:11).

The joy we have here is fleeting; we fight to hold on to it in the midst of painful trials and the mundane routines of everyday life. It can't compare to the fullness of joy found in His presence. His joy is abundant and overflowing and satisfying. His very presence, with its complete joy, is our inheritance, and it's beautiful.

Lord, my heart is filled to overflowing with joy at the thought of the beautiful inheritance that awaits me.

East Meets West

As far as the east is from the west,
so far has he removed our transgressions from us.

You're standing on the surface of the earth at point A. Draw an imaginary line around the earth to point B. Now imagine that you set off on a journey from point A, traveling east. If you continue eastward, at what point would you no longer be traveling east? The answer is point B. Since the earth is round, from that point on you'd be traveling west, back toward point A.

People in the time of David, who wrote Psalm 103, didn't know the earth is round like a sphere; they still believed the earth was flat. Therefore, David pictured God throwing our sins away, and those sins going east forever, never reaching a point where they'd circle back toward us. He pictured them being flung into eternity—out of sight, out of mind, forever.

Few things can spark joy like the knowledge that when God forgives, it's a forever deal. Forgiven offenses will *never* come back to us.

Lord, I'm so grateful that when You forgive, You forgive completely and forever.

Justice

For the LORD is righteous, he loves justice.

—Psalm 11:7

f God were just, you think, *He wouldn't allow _____.*

Whoa, there! How do *we* know what God would or wouldn't do? How do we—finite human beings—know what's truly just and what isn't?

Thought patterns like this one can rob us of joy. But if we really believe God, and truly believe that He's all-good and all-knowing, then we can also rest in His Word. The Bible tells us He "loves justice." If He loves justice, would He be unjust? God is merciful, yes, but He's also supremely just. Unlike us humans, God doesn't just *think* something's right, or good, or just, He *knows* when it is! Because He's a perfect God, every decision He makes is perfect.

While we live here on earth, we have very limited knowledge and understanding. There are many, many things, such as the justice of God, that we won't fully understand until we're in heaven. Until then, we can completely trust that God's ways are flawless.

Lord, I'm filled with joy at the thought that You always know—and You always do—what's right and fair and just.

An Experiment

My children, listen to me, for all who follow my ways are joyful.
—Proverbs 8:32 NLT

Do you feel weighed down before you even crawl out of bed in the morning? Is it difficult to remember the last time you had a carefree day? If so, try an experiment. For one day, live as though God loves you like crazy and you have nothing to fear. At first, you might feel a little silly (like you're acting or pretending), but stay with it. No matter what you do that day, do it as though you're utterly loved by God and have no worries whatsoever. Soon you'll discover you're breathing easier. You might have more energy or enjoy your workday more than usual. Laughter will come more easily.

The beauty of this little experiment is that, since the imagination is a powerful thing, you'll have moments when you forget you're "just pretending." You'll feel genuine joy . . . contentment . . . peace. At the end of the day, say to yourself, *That's the life I was meant to lead.* And then pursue that life; since you're completely loved by the One who says, "Fear not," it's yours for the taking!

Lord, I want to live each day in the joy and the truth that You love me completely, and I have nothing to fear.

The Lord's Protection

He will cover you with his feathers, and under his wings you will find refuge; his faithfulness will be your shield.

—Psalm 91:4

What makes you feel safe and protected? Is it an alarm system, having someone else in the house, or maybe a pet of some kind? The problem with any of these sources of protection is that they're fallible. An alarm system could break, a person can fall asleep, and a dog may not react in the way we hoped.

It's fascinating that the psalmist didn't say that God's strength will protect us. He didn't say that we'll find our security in His omniscience, omnipresence, or holiness. Our security, he said, comes from the faithfulness of God.

We can rejoice in the Lord's promise to protect us (Psalm 121:5) because we also have the promise of His faithfulness (2 Timothy 2:13). These are more than words or warm, fuzzy feelings; faithfulness is at the heart of God's character. There is joy in knowing that His faithfulness and His protection are inseparable.

Whatever comes my way, Father, I'll rejoice knowing that You've covered me with Your faithfulness.

The Joy of Being Chosen

Remember the wonders he has done . . . you his servants . . . his
chosen ones, the children of Jacob.

—Psalm 105:5–6

When you were in elementary school, did you ever try to look as invisible as possible because you were afraid the teacher would call on you to answer a difficult question? You slumped your shoulders and refused to make eye contact, hoping he wouldn't choose you. Sometimes we try to avoid being chosen, but other times we want it very much. Being chosen right off the bat for a game of touch football at a family picnic is enjoyable. Perhaps you've experienced the pleasure of being named Employee of the Year.

Or maybe you've been passed over a few too many times. If you're a Christian, however, you can live joyfully in the knowledge that you were chosen by the God of the universe. He not only created you and laid out the plan for who you'd be and where you'd live, He picked you. You are the chosen child of God. No one can change that.

Lord, You didn't have to choose me, create me, or love me, but
You've done all three, and that makes me so happy!

Joy in the Lord's Company

Therefore, if anyone is united with the Anointed One, that person is a new creation.

—2 Corinthians 5:17 VOICE

Has anyone ever said to you, "Well, I can certainly tell you've been hanging out with So-and-So." Maybe the person said it as a compliment: after a week visiting your sister, who loves to bake, you came home and whipped up a red velvet cake. Or maybe it was a criticism: after one Boy's Night Out with a certain friend, you suddenly need your mouth washed out with soap. Either way, the principle is the same: we become like those we spend the most time with.

God created joy. (Even more accurately, He *is* joy.) He also created laughter and humor. (Surely only a God with a sense of humor would create anteaters, giraffes, and Jack Russell terriers.) It stands to reason that when we spend time in His company, joy and humor will rub off on us.

Are you lacking joy this week? Stop and talk for a while with the God of joy.

Lord, I could use an extra dose of joy today. Can we hang out for a while? I need You to rub off on me.

Our Unchanging God

"I the Lord do not change."

—Malachi 3:6

Do you sometimes feel the world is changing so quickly you can't keep up? Even our own language is morphing at an unprecedented rate. In just the past two years, the major dictionaries have added several thousand words, many of which reflect changes in culture and technology: *Vlog, hangry, awesomesauce,* and *cafe cat. Melty, cupcakery, M'kay, clickbait, emoji,* and *photobomb.*

Meanwhile, our opinions are almost as fleeting as everything else. One minute we're dyed-in-the-wool Android fans, and the next minute we won't settle for anything but an iPhone. So many changes—so quickly!—can get confusing and throw even the most adaptable person off balance.

Our consolation as Christians is that God is wholly stable and unchanging. Better yet, His opinions don't change. He was "all about" us even before we were born, and He still feels the same way. Even when we're fickle, He's not.

Oh, the joy of belonging to a God who's constant!

Thank You, Lord, that even when everything—including me—seems unpredictable and fickle, You never change.

Part of the Family

You are citizens along with all of God's holy people. You are members of God's family.

—Ephesians 2:19 NLT

amily members sometimes drive one another a bit crazy. Mothers and daughters squabble, siblings can find it difficult to see eye to eye, and fathers and sons often butt heads over the best way to do something. Still, families are bound in a way that no other people group can replicate. The feeling of belonging, the comfort of traditions, and the ease of long-term relationships all bring deep joy.

No wonder we enjoy getting together with our kingdom family. No, we don't share the same DNA, but we share the same Father, the same destiny, and an eternal bond that can't be shaken. Do you smile from ear to ear when you meet with your Bible study group on Thursday evenings? Do you feel a surge of joy when you walk into church on Sunday? Let your family know! "I'm so happy to see you. I just love being around you!"

Lord, thank You that You've given me spiritual brothers, sisters, mothers, fathers, and children. Help me to love them well.

Holiday Harmony

Show family affection to one another. . . . Outdo one another in showing honor.

—Romans 12:10 HCSB

November and December are filled with cultural traditions, many of which we hold very dear: turkey, gravy, and cranberry sauce. Nativity scenes, twinkling lights, and carols—many cultural traditions are lovely and worth protecting.

On the other hand, as you prepare for the festivities to come, keep in mind that a person can squeeze the joy right out of the holidays by insisting on doing things the way they've always been done. As your kids get older and start their own families, or if you're part of a blended family, leave room for something new. Mentally separate "nonessential" from "nonnegotiable." For example, trading turkey and dressing for some other menu that might suit the vegetarian in-laws might be unthinkable, but incorporating a few vegetable-based dishes will go a long way toward family harmony. And remember that new traditions can become just as joyful as the old ones if you compromise and remember the true meaning behind the holidays. Let's live out the verse above and "outdo one another in showing honor."

Lord, help me remember that the holidays aren't all about me. Help me honor others rather than drain the joy out of this season by insisting on my own way.

The Mystery

This message was kept secret for centuries and generations past, but now it has been revealed to God's people.

—Colossians 1:26 NLT

Who doesn't love a good mystery? Whether you're playing the board game Clue or attending a dinner theater, it's always fun to be the one who puts the clues together and solves the mystery. By reading the Old Testament, we see a beautiful mystery unfold. We see clues given and hints dropped.

Paul described the coming Messiah as a mystery hidden for ages. For generations prophets had been given only glimpses of the glory, and the people held only pieces to the puzzle. Then Jesus was born, the mystery was revealed, and all of heaven rejoiced (Luke 2:13).

How can we not live joyfully knowing that the mystery, which so many longed to understand, has been revealed to us (Colossians 2:2)? Not only was it revealed to us, but it resides in us (Colossians 1:27). Every clue points to Christ, and every prophecy finds its fulfillment in Him. Let's live each day rejoicing that God chose to reveal His Son to us.

Thank You, Lord, for revealing the mystery of Jesus to me.

Your Name Is Written

"However, don't rejoice that the spirits submit to you, but rejoice that your names are written in heaven."

—Luke 10:20 HCSB

God gives amazing abilities to people. Whether we're a neurosurgeon, a top-notch cook, or a poet, our gifts bring us a lot of pleasure and joy. Perhaps we're even tempted to boast about them.

When Jesus sent out the seventy-two, He gave them some amazing abilities. They were able to proclaim the gospel, heal the sick, and cast out demons. When they returned to Jesus they could hardly contain their excitement (Luke 10:17). He was quick to point out that He was the One who instilled the power in them; they were rejoicing over the wrong thing.

God gives good gifts (Matthew 7:11) and we're clearly supposed to enjoy and share them, but our talents can't be the source of our joy. Any of our earthly abilities could be gone in an instant. Jesus pointed the excited followers (and us) to the Father, in whom true joy should be found. Those who trust Christ can rejoice knowing their names have been written in the Book of Life, and that can never be taken away.

Lord, teach me to use my gifts for Your glory while keeping in mind the greatest joy: that my name is written in heaven.

The Word of the Lord

"It is the same with my word. I send it out, and it always produces fruit. It will accomplish all I want it to, and it will prosper everywhere I send it."

—Isaiah 55:11 NLT

Have you ever said something and not received the response you expected? Perhaps your apology wasn't accepted or your declaration of love wasn't reciprocated. Maybe your request wasn't honored or your comment was ignored. What if your every word accomplished exactly what you intended?

God's Word always accomplishes what He sends it out to do. Every word in Scripture has a purpose and will never go forth in vain. In fact, the Lord promises that His Word will always produce fruit. Think about that in terms of sharing the gospel with people around you.

We don't have to concern ourselves with results. The fact is that there will be times when people won't listen (Ezekiel 3:7), but that's not our concern. We can still share His Word with joy. We can plant and water the seed, freely knowing that God grants the harvest and the crop will be exactly what He intended (1 Corinthians 3:6–7).

Lord, I believe that Your Word is alive and active. I rejoice that it will accomplish Your will and will prosper wherever You send it.

Signs and Symbols

Here am I, and the children the LORD has given me. We are signs and symbols in Israel from the LORD Almighty, who dwells on Mount Zion.

—Isaiah 8:18

Have you ever gone through a time when your definition of success was just making it through the day? There are seasons when we're waiting for God to move in some way and to make His presence known. Everything seems hot and dry, and we're desperate for something to refresh us.

The prophet Isaiah knew a little something about waiting. Things were difficult, and God was hiding His face from the house of Jacob. But Isaiah refused to lose faith. He was determined to stand his ground and continue to hope. He was so committed to His God that he offered himself and his children as signs of warning and hope that would point others to the God who still ruled in Zion.

There can be joy even in the midst of the driest season. We can have hope no matter what fear and hysteria the world attempts to instill in our hearts. By living with joy, we can be signs and symbols that point others to the God who has not relinquished control.

My family and I will live with joy, Lord, and guide others to the eternal hope found in You.

Draw with Joy

With joy you will draw water from the wells of salvation.

—Isaiah 12:3

Where do you turn for relief when the world weighs you down? There are times when our faith seems frail and our spirits are dry. We need a place to go, a well to draw from, to refresh and revitalize our souls.

The Samaritan woman of John 4 had undoubtedly drawn water from the well countless times. Each day looked just like the one before it: draw the water, carry the water, use the water. It refreshed for a moment but always left her wanting and needing more, so she would go back. With weariness she would draw from the well again, knowing it was a temporary solution to a continuing need.

The well of salvation is different; it offers permanent relief. There's joy for the one who draws from this well because it quenches the thirsty soul forever (John 4:14). The one who draws from the well of salvation is forever refreshed.

I drank from the world's well for too long, Lord, and it always left me thirsting for more. Thank You for Your abundant well of salvation.

Pure in Heart

"Blessed are the pure in heart, for they will see God."

—Matthew 5:8

Have you ever misjudged someone based on appearances? This is a common mistake that people have been making from the beginning (1 Samuel 16:7). The condition of a person's heart isn't easily determined by observing him or her with our eyes.

Jewish tradition put great emphasis on rules and rituals; the focus was on external purity. A person had to do good, be good, and have the right heritage. What you wore, what you ate, and whom you associated with all mattered in terms of your alleged closeness to God. The reality was that none of the laws and traditions allowed even the most ceremonially pure to see God.

Jesus completely flipped the script on the Pharisees when He called the pure in heart "blessed." This opened the floodgates as to who could "see God." Appearances, family history, prior mistakes—none of it matters. This should make us all shout for joy; we are made pure through the Lamb and shall one day see God.

Thank You, Lord, for seeing beyond my messes and mistakes. I can live with joy knowing that You look upon my heart.

Gift of His Word

I rejoice at your word like one who finds great spoil.

—Psalm 119:162 ESV

How many Bibles do you currently have in your home? Most of us probably have multiple copies, and we certainly could go online or walk into any number of stores to purchase more if we desired. When is the last time you picked up the Word of God and rejoiced as if you had found hidden treasure?

A video has been circulating for years of the Kimya tribe in Indonesia receiving the Bible in their own language. The people of the tribe gather as the plane containing the shipment arrives. There are singing, dancing, and tears of joy as a time of pure celebration breaks out for the men, women, and children of the tribe.

Many of us are guilty of treating the Word of God very casually. How much joy could be added to our lives if we would recognize the gift of Scripture? What if we celebrated like the Kimya people over God's Word?

Your Word is one long love letter from You to me, Lord. I'll rejoice at the message of love within it.

The Joy of Remembering

But whoever looks intently into the perfect law that gives freedom,
and continues in it—not forgetting what they have heard, but doing
it—they will be blessed in what they do.

—James 1:25

ave you ever been listening to the radio when an old song came on and you thought, *I forgot how much I love this kind of music!* Many of us say something similar on Thanksgiving when we take that first bite of hot turkey: "Why don't I cook turkey all year long? I forget how much I enjoy it."

Once we start neglecting the Word of God, we tend to forget how much we love it. We forget how much life and light it adds to our day. Then we finally (almost grudgingly) open our Bible again, and within minutes we're sighing with relief: *Ahhhhhh. Why don't I do this more often?*

In the above verse, James admonished his readers to "look intently into the perfect law" and then *continue* to do so. *The Voice* translation explains that by doing so you'll "avoid the many distractions that lead to an amnesia of all true things and you will be blessed."

Feast on the Word today, and the next day, and the next . . . and your joy will continue.

Forgive me, Lord, for being so forgetful about how much I love Your
Word. Increase my hunger for You and the Scriptures.

Oh, Happiness!

Great grace was on all of them.

—Acts 4:33 HCSB

Some believers get a kick out of shopping with friends or family on Black Friday. Others envision the crowds, traffic, and long lines, and avoid going out altogether. Regardless of our shopping preferences, many of us are disheartened that certain stores now open for sales on Thanksgiving Day, and we have a difficult time understanding what would motivate some bargain hunters to tent camp outside their favorite department stores through the night.

These overenthusiastic shoppers have set their sights on a certain toy or electronic device and made up their minds to snag one before they're all gone. They're spurred to drastic measures by the fear that there aren't enough of the best items to go around. This might be true in the material world, but it's completely false in the spiritual one: the treasures that matter most are never in short supply. When our hearts are set on things like God's endless grace, love, and truth, we can revel in the happiness and the grace that have been given to everyone.

Thank You, Lord, that joy, love, grace, and truth are never going to run out!

Unity

How good and pleasant it is when God's people live together in unity!

—Psalm 133:1

Whether children in a family, coworkers in an office, or the Philippian church in Paul's day (Philippians 2:2), everyone experiences more joy when they're living in unity with one another. We live in a world where people feel obligated to share their every opinion on a vast array of subjects. Disagreements on trivial matters can cause unnecessary divisions.

David knew division was unacceptable for God's people. To live joyfully, we must learn to get along with others. It's good to live in unity with people who look different and have different gifts. We can have varying opinions on church music or methods but still live in agreement on Jesus. How good and pleasant it is when we focus on the areas where we agree!

Paul warned believers to avoid people who caused dissension (Romans 16:17), and Solomon listed a person who spreads strife among the things that the Lord hated (Proverbs 6:16, 19). Let's seek to live in unity with fellow believers so we can all live more joyfully.

Forgive me, Lord, for the times when I've been a source of division. Help me to enjoy the good and pleasant fruit of living in unity.

The House of the Lord

I was glad when they said to me, "Let us go to the house of the LORD!"

—Psalm 122:1 ESV

Those of us responsible for getting our families dressed and to church on time know that Lionel Richie had it wrong: there's nothing easy about Sunday morning. We rush to get ready, slide into the pew just in time, and—if we're lucky—count our blessings that no one got into an argument on the way there.

Many of us take for granted what made David glad. How much more joy would be in your life if you rejoiced at the opportunity to go to the house of the Lord each week? David saw it for what it was: a privilege, and not simply another optional activity on a given day.

In order to live more joyfully, let's begin rejoicing when it's time to join fellow believers in worship. Whether a weekly service, a special event, or a time of fellowship, let's sincerely be glad to be in the Lord's house spending time with His people. There's joy in the house of the Lord.

Lord, it's a joy to gather in Your house for worship. I will enter Your courts with thanksgiving and praise.

Live in the Lord

So now, my little children, live in Him.

—1 John 2:28 VOICE

For many couples and friends, the most joyful moments are those spent sitting in each other's company, sometimes without even speaking. The more time we spend with our friend Jesus, the more we'll find that sometimes He, too, simply wants to hang out with us. He loves our company and wants us to learn to be content and joyful in His. Christianity is a far less complicated way of life than you might believe—minus the frenzy and busyness that make up much of what we call Christianity these days.

Until we learn to "live in Him," silence and simplicity might make us uncomfortable. This is why some believers have an easier time obeying God when He tells them to take on a complex project than when He says, "Come sit on your bed and just be with Me." So the next time you feel a nudge to pull yourself away from whatever you're doing and just *be*, rejoice that the Lord is calling You, and answer Him quickly!

Lord, I want to learn to be completely joyful and content in Your company—and quick to stop and be with You when You call.

The God Who Sees Us

The LORD looks down from heaven and sees the whole human race.
—Psalm 33:13 NLT

There's a trendy little street in Forest Park, Illinois, where one can stand on the sidewalk, look point-blank east, and see Chicago's Sears Tower as clearly as if it were a mile or two away—when in fact, it's ten miles as the crow flies. This is because, as the second-tallest building in the country, it stands 108 stories high. It's always there, even when shrouded temporarily by rain or fog. In Chicago, numerous buildings qualify as skyscrapers, but the Tower surpasses all others and "keeps watch" on city dwellers and suburbanites many miles away.

Does this remind you of God, in whose shadow we're always safe, and who has His eye on us even when we can't feel His presence? No wonder David Crowder wrote of this immense but intimate God when he discussed that sometimes God feels as close to us as our skin, while other times He feels as distant from us as the moon. Don't think it strange when you're going about your business and you suddenly have a joyful awareness of His closeness. Thank Him for being near, and enjoy His presence.

No matter where I am, You always have Your eye on me—every minute of every day. Thank You, Lord!

The Joy of Pure Conversation

For the Scriptures say, "If you want to enjoy life and see many happy days, keep your tongue from speaking evil and your lips from telling lies."

—1 Peter 3:10 NLT

This verse explains that a long, joyful life is one that's free of sinful conversation. But these days, steering clear of toxic discussions and foul language can be a real challenge. Flip the remote for ten seconds and you'll witness violence, distasteful jokes, and far too much skin. Even so, we can't escape verses like Ephesians 5:12: "It is shameful even to mention what the disobedient do in secret." *Really?* we might think. *I shouldn't even* talk *about certain sins?* This verse clearly cautions us against discussing (much less watching) roughly a thousand and one popular TV shows.

God wasn't being unreasonable when He set these parameters. He knows how quickly we can slip away from a place of peace, purity, and joy. And when we see and hear so much filth, we can become desensitized, even when we genuinely desire to be holy, as God called us to be.

Let's love the world and the people in it while also keeping ourselves free from the kind of talk that steals our joy.

I want to please You with the way I talk and the things I talk about, Lord. Rein me in when my conversations wander into shark-infested waters!

The Joy of Answered Prayer

He lifted me out of the slimy pit, out of the mud and mire; he set my feet on a rock and gave me a firm place to stand.

—Psalm 40:2

He'd been a hunter from an early age and knew his way around in the woods. What he didn't expect, however, was that the "dry" riverbed he was about to cross was riddled with quicksand. A few steps in, he found himself sinking into the mire. Knowing that no one was within hearing, and also knowing that struggling would sink him more deeply, he began praying. It was then that he noticed a large tree nearby, with one low branch. Trying not to move unnecessarily, he grabbed for the branch—and missed. He prayed harder. Again he reached for the branch; it was just out of his reach. He cried out to God, trusting Him to help him. He'd give it one more try.

Back home, the young man's mother—who knew nothing of his predicament—was praying Psalm 40 over him. She looked at the clock. It was 9:10 a.m.

On his third try, he caught the branch. Praying it would hold him, he pulled himself out of the mire and headed joyfully for home. It was 9:10 a.m.

What joy it brings to my heart knowing that, in any situation, I can trust You to help me, Lord!

DECEMBER

With the Lord

Then we who are alive, who are left, will be caught up together with them in the clouds to meet the Lord in the air, and so we will always be with the Lord.

—1 Thessalonians 4:17 ESV

Who's that person whose mere presence makes you glad? You look forward to being with this person, and you think about him often when he's gone. You treasure each moment together so that you can replay every detail later in your mind.

We read about a certain beggar in Mark 5 who desperately needed something from Jesus. He had been possessed by demons, rejected by people, and lived chained among the tombs. The man needed the healing hand of Christ, but when all was said and done, healing wasn't enough. The man wanted to remain in the presence of Jesus (Mark 5:18). In fact, Scripture says that he *begged* the Lord to allow him to go with Him.

There are many things we receive at the Lord's hands, but none of them compare to the time when we'll finally be able to remain in His presence forever. Whatever today may hold, we can look forward with joy to that day.

Lord, I'm so grateful for the healing I've received at Your hand, but I long for the day when I can remain in Your presence forever.

The Multitude

They all ate and were satisfied. Afterward the disciples picked up seven basketfuls of broken pieces that were left over.

—Matthew 15:37

Sometimes we focus our eyes too intently on the visible. We get all caught up in our circumstances and forget that we serve a mighty God whose power knows no limits. We look at the problems around us and decide that they're insurmountable. Even the disciples were guilty of underestimating God (Matthew 15:33).

These men had been following Christ. They'd listened to His teachings and witnessed His healings. Yet when it came to feeding the multitude before them, they were quick to consider it an impossible job. They looked at the crowd, looked at their food supply, and concluded that it would never work.

Just as these disciples discovered, we can rejoice knowing that God is more than enough for any need. When He fills our cups, they overflow (Psalm 23:5). Sometimes God does more than show up; He shows off His glory. Let's live with joy as we remember the bigness of our God.

I'm in awe of the way You provide, Lord. Your gifts are always in abundance; Your generosity knows no bounds.

What Is Not Seen

Now faith is the reality of what is hoped for, the proof of what is not seen.

—Hebrews 11:1 HCSB

Have you ever found it difficult to see beyond the current storm? It's easy to focus on the things most visible—the trials surrounding us. When we focus on the things immediately in front of us, we lose sight of things that are eternal.

A person who lives with joy has a faith that sees past the battle of the day. It's a faith that enables a person to say, regardless of loss or devastation, "My God promised." We must hope in what we can't see and place our trust in the Word of the Almighty (Proverbs 30:5).

If we'll endure to the end, we'll have the same testimony as Caleb (Joshua 14:10). We'll look back with gladness, recall all of the Lord's blessings, and declare to all that God did as He promised. Now, we live by faith (2 Corinthians 5:7); one day, we'll live by sight and we'll praise the One who kept every promise.

God, I'll trust in what I can't see. I look forward to the day when I joyfully declare that my God did just as He promised.

Unknown Paths

"I will lead the blind by ways they have not known, along unfamiliar paths I will guide them."

—Isaiah 42:16

If you've ever uttered the words, "I have no idea what I'm doing," you know the helplessness that can accompany them. Whether you're caring for an aging parent, parenting a strong-willed child, or navigating any number of life's unexpected paths, feeling completely unprepared can be frightening.

There's a beautiful promise for every believer when it comes to those uncharted territories in our lives. God Himself promises to be our tour guide. If you feel lost, He'll lead the way. If you've never been in this place before, He'll guide you.

The enemy wants you to mistake *inexperienced* for *ill-equipped*. He'd love for you to stumble along and grasp anything that looks like it might lead you through your crisis. But you can rejoice knowing that your tour guide is the One who created it all, and He's more than capable of safely guiding you home.

I will not fear when I encounter new paths, Lord. I'll joyfully follow wherever You lead me.

God's Confidant

*The LORD confides in those who fear him; he makes his covenant
known to them.*

—Psalm 25:14

You're reading the Bible when you come across a passage you just can't understand. You struggle to make sense of it, to no avail. Wait! Don't you know you have a tool—free of charge, easily accessible, and guaranteed to work—that'll help make the passage clear? Pray! Ask God to clarify it; ask Him for a revelation about it. He might not give you an answer immediately, but He *will* answer you . . . if you fear (revere) Him.

Some of God's promises in the Bible are if/then promises: they're granted under certain circumstances. This is one of them. Before your friend will tell you a secret, she wants to be sure she can trust you to keep it. Likewise, God wants to know you truly fear Him before He'll reveal certain secrets to you. That might sound restrictive, but imagine the joy you'll experience when our awesome God tells you a secret that He'll reveal only to chosen people! (And imagine the joy when you finally understand that troublesome passage!)

*Thank You, God, that You hear and answer my prayers. Thank You
that You reveal Your secrets to me!*

Plans for Your Child

"For I know the plans I have for you," declares the LORD, "plans to prosper you and not to harm you, plans to give you hope and a future."

—Jeremiah 29:11

Every parent of a newborn infant begins thinking about that child's future. Will he or she be a doctor, a teacher, a farmer? Foremost in every parent's mind, however, should be the question, *Will my child one day enter the kingdom of heaven?*

In the book of Jeremiah, God says He knew you "before [He] formed you in the womb" (1:5). Then God goes on to say He knew the plans He had for you. His plans were "to give you hope and a future"—in other words, to see you come into His kingdom. It gives the Lord great joy to see us become children of God: "There is rejoicing in the presence of the angels of God over one sinner who repents" (Luke 15:10).

Admittedly, parents have little control over what their children will do when they grow up. We do, however, know this: the surest way for a parent to find joy is to raise up a righteous child!

Lord, thank You that even before I was born, You planned for me to one day enter Your kingdom. Help us to raise our children to become children of God.

A Joyful Transition

"Hey, Death! Where is your big win? Hey, Grave! What happened to your sting?"

—Hosea 13:14 VOICE

You're driving and daydreaming when suddenly you round a corner and there it is: an expanse of mountain range so beautiful you gasp out loud. One minute you're whiling away the miles, and the next you are, it seems, in an altogether different place—a perfect, magnificent world.

For the Christian, this is what the transition from this life to the next will be like. Death—that event that so many people spend so much time and energy fretting about—does not get the last say. Jesus made sure of that. Granted, few people look forward to dying, and losing a loved one is among the most sorrowful things that can happen to a person, but the power of death to completely snuff out life ended when Jesus rose from the grave. The moment after we take our last breath on earth, we'll see a new and spectacular vista in heaven, and what a joyful moment that will be!

Lord, thank You for taking the sting out of death. Thank You for having the last say and giving me life everlasting.

The Joy of Mentoring

And the things you have heard me say . . . entrust to reliable people who will also be qualified to teach others.

—2 Timothy 2:2

One of the best things about growing older and having some experience under our belts is the ability to pass on that hard-earned wisdom and knowledge through mentoring. We don't hear much about mentoring these days, but it's just as crucial as ever, and perhaps more so in our unstable and competitive world.

I don't have much to offer, you might say. But consider your interests in different areas of your life.

Physical: teach someone to follow in your footsteps by taking care of herself physically—for example, guide her through a "Couch to 5K" program.

Relational: pass on your skills as a spouse by mentoring a young husband or wife who's having trouble adjusting to putting someone else first.

Professional: share your knowledge of auto repair, leadership traits, or resume writing.

Spiritual: impart the riches that God has imparted to you with a hungry young soul.

Discover the joy of mentoring.

Show me, Lord, if there's anyone in my circle of influence who's longing to learn what You've taught me over the years.

The Joy of Friendship

The righteous choose their friends carefully.

—Proverbs 12:26

harles Swindoll said, "I cannot even imagine where I would be today were it not for that handful of friends who have given me a heart full of joy." If you have friends, thank God for them, and then thank Him again! They're a great treasure.

Sometimes we go through seasons that are lacking in close relationships, and this isn't necessarily our fault at all. But other times we might lack friends because we're not being proactive. Sometimes we isolate ourselves; we don't mean to be unfriendly, but relationships take energy and time, and by the end of the workday we're so tired we just want to go home and collapse in front our favorite Netflix series.

If you've lost touch with old friends, make a point of getting together. If you could use a few new friends, take part in a group activity once in a while, whether a hiking club, church group, or volunteer opportunity. And don't wait passively for others to approach you; introduce yourself. You never know—you might be the answer to someone else's prayer for a true friend!

Lord, thank You so much for the friends I have, and please lead me to anyone else You want me to befriend this week.

Satisfied with God

Keep your lives free from the love of money.

—Hebrews 13:5

Plenty of couples who've celebrated a fiftieth wedding anniversary will tell you they'd do it all over again, right down to the ceremony—even when that ceremony cost next to nothing. Sometimes the coziest, most welcoming home is the smallest and humblest one on the block. Many people can attest to making lifelong memories with their families while tent camping versus staying in five-star hotels.

The level of joy in one's life is not contingent on the state of his or her bank account. This isn't to say money is inherently bad: having enough to go around can relieve stress and make certain experiences possible that you might otherwise miss. But some of the "poorest of the poor" experience joy in their everyday lives simply because their hearts are satisfied with God and what He's given them, regardless of how modest it is.

If you're waiting for your finances to straighten themselves out so you can be happy, stop focusing on your bank account and turn your attention to the joy-giver Himself.

Lord, forgive me for thinking that money can buy joy. I receive all that You have for me right here, right now.

Magnify

Oh, magnify the LORD with me, and let us exalt his name together!
—Psalm 34:3 ESV

Isn't it amazing how, when you look at something through a simple magnifying glass, little details that weren't visible with the naked eye suddenly become clear? In the same way, when you magnify the Lord, you'll see little details about Him that you weren't able to see or understand earlier.

God loves it when we worship, praise, glorify, and magnify Him and His holy name. He inhabits the praises of His people. Consequently, when we worship, praise, glorify, and magnify Him, we bring Him great joy; He is closer to us then than He is at any other time, and He'll even reveal more about Himself to us . . . hence, the small revelations about Him that we'll see! Prayer, praise, and worship are the great "magnifying glasses" that bring God closer to us, that reveal hidden things about His character to us, and that fill both Him and us with joy.

I lift my voice to You in praise and worship for who You are. Come closer to me, God, my Father; I long to know You better.

Seeking Joy

For you have been my help, and in the shadow of your wings I will sing for joy.

—Psalm 63:7 ESV

How do you handle the heat? Typically, there are two types of people. There are those who can bask on the beach, soak in the sun, and enjoy every minute of it. Then there are those who hunker down in front of a box fan from June through August. The only way they can find joy at the beach is to position themselves under one of those lovely beach umbrellas.

Here's the thing about those beach umbrellas: in order to take advantage of the protection they offer, you have to sit pretty close to them. The same goes for those of us who wish to seek shelter within the shadow of the Almighty; we must remain close to Him. Only then can we partake of His protection. Are you seeking some joy in the midst of the heat of the day? Scoot a little closer to the shade.

Thank You, Lord, for allowing us to get so close to You that we can rest and find joy in Your shadow.

Power of Christ

But he said to me, "My grace is sufficient for you, for my power is made perfect in weakness." Therefore I will boast all the more gladly about my weaknesses, so that Christ's power may rest on me.
—2 Corinthians 12:9

When was the last time you bragged about something that caused you to struggle? People don't naturally boast about their weaknesses. None of us want our shortcomings broadcast for others to critique and judge. We edit our stories and our pictures so that no one knows our struggles. It's an exhausting way to live.

After begging God to remove a certain weakness of his, Paul discovered an amazing gift: human weaknesses offer opportunities for God to work wonders. By letting go of pride, we make room for the power of Christ to rest on us. Can you think of anything more joyful than walking around with the power of Christ upon you?

In what areas do you feel inadequate? What is it that you, like Paul, have pleaded with God to change? Rejoice—the perfect power of Christ can do an amazing thing with your weakness.

I want Your power to rest on me, Lord. Help me to be content in my weaknesses so that I may witness You at work in my life.

Joyful Light

When they saw the star, they were overjoyed.

—Matthew 2:10

How many times have you been overjoyed by a light? There are night-lights that comfort us in the middle of the night and porch lights that welcome us home. Many of us have felt the excitement of spotting a car's headlights when waiting for someone's arrival or the thrill of Christmas lights during the holidays.

Lights have been bringing joy from the very beginning. When the star that signaled the birth of the Messiah shone, the joy the Magi felt caused them to make a journey. There was something about that light.

Of all the ways God could have signaled the coming of His Son, He chose to send a light into the darkness. He knew the joy that a light can bring to a weary heart, and the star was just a glimpse of the joy to come. There's still a Light who causes people to be overjoyed. The light of Christ can bring comfort on the darkest night and can thrill a soul like no other (John 8:12).

You've been dispelling darkness and bringing light from the very beginning, Lord. I'm overjoyed that I've seen Your light.

Complete Joy

We write this to make our joy complete.

—1 John 1:4

ost of us get a kick out of sharing good news. Can you think of a time when you could hardly wait to share something you'd witnessed or learned with someone you know? Telling someone else good news brings joy to everyone involved.

You've surely heard the saying *Love isn't love until you give it away*. For John, joy wasn't complete until it was shared. John was an eyewitness to the life and ministry of Christ (1 John 1:1), and he wanted to share what he knew so that everyone's joy could be complete.

As believers, we should feel compelled to share what we've seen and heard (Acts 4:20). God has done amazing things in all of our lives; let's not keep our stories to ourselves. We'll spread joy to others and experience more joy ourselves when we make it our mission to proclaim what we know to be true of Christ.

I'll speak of Your wonders in my life, Lord. I can't help but tell of what I've seen You do.

Our Prayers Are Heard

Before I finished praying in my heart, Rebekah came out.

—Genesis 24:45

We need to know that God hears us. Have you ever felt as if your whispered pleas for mercy have gone unanswered? Have you ever wondered how you were supposed to know if the answer was *No* or *Not yet*? Finding the answers to our prayers can seem confusing until we pick up His Word and let Him speak.

It's hard to comprehend how God can answer our prayer before we've even finished praying it. But time is different for Him. God is not overwhelmed by the ticking of the clock; He feels no panic at the passing of the years.

The nature of our request or need doesn't matter. We can have joy knowing it's already been answered in Him. We're never being ignored by our heavenly Father. Instead, the silence is an indication that there's nothing further that needs to be handled. It's already been tended to, and we no longer need to carry the weight of worry.

Before you whispered your request through weary lips, He already knew (Matthew 6:32). When it was still a silent hope hidden deep in the heart, He had already answered. We can live joyfully knowing that God has not lost track of time. Our prayers have been heard.

You hear my every prayer, Lord, as well as the ones I don't even know to pray. Thank You for being a God who hears.

First Love

"But I have this against you, that you have abandoned the love you had at first."

—Revelation 2:4 ESV

Do you ever do good things with a bad attitude? Everyone has, at some point, been guilty of this. We take the right action and hope God notices, but on the inside we're complaining. We're grumbling, envious, and slightly sick of it all. God notices when we live our lives full of negativity.

There's no joy in doing things this way—not even right things. We get joy only when we do things out of love, because love is a big deal to God (1 Corinthians 13:13), and we should make it our goal to be like Him.

In order to live joyfully, our actions must be an overflow of the love we have inside of us for God and for one another. Let's take the time to examine our hearts and our motives. Anything done out of obligation will fail to reap the harvest of joy we desire.

Lord, restore to me the love I had at first so my motives may be pure and my heart can rejoice.

Overwhelmed

From the ends of the earth I call to you, I call as my heart grows
faint; lead me to the rock that is higher than I.

—Psalm 61:2

Do you ever feel overwhelmed by the stage of life you're in right now? One day you feel as if you have everything under control. Then, little by little, the ground begins to give way beneath you. Before you know it, you're in over your head.

Satan will take these difficult stages and try to convince you that God simply didn't equip you well enough for this season of life. He'll try to replace your joy with anxiety and fear. The psalmist knew that to maintain our joy when life is overwhelming, we must run to the Rock.

To live joyfully, we must know where to turn; we must be students of Scripture (2 Timothy 3:16–17). Staying in the Word will enable us to rejoice, knowing that we're thoroughly equipped for every task. There will be days when the waters rise, but long before Satan has a chance to pull us under, let's cry out to the One who's never overwhelmed.

Lord, I won't let the enemy steal my joy. I'll turn to You and Your
Word when life becomes too much for me to handle.

Work with Joy

So I saw that there is nothing better for a person than to enjoy their work.

—Ecclesiastes 3:22

Do you begin your week with the Monday morning blues, or do you look forward to the start of a new week? Do you find yourself trudging your way through the workweek and then attempting to cram as much fun as possible into Saturday and Sunday? We've probably all been guilty of working for the weekend occasionally.

Whether we find ourselves doing what we always dreamed of or not, it was never God's intention that we endure five days, enjoy two days, and then start all over again. Solomon tried many ways to find meaning and satisfaction with his life, but in the end, this man, known for his wisdom, declared that there was "nothing better for a person than to enjoy their work."

How can we find joy in our day-to-day work? First, we can view it as a gift instead of a grind. We can bring our Father glory by working diligently, loving others well, and seeking opportunities to serve. When we work in a way that honors the Lord, we will find a joy we did not see before.

Teach me, Lord, to see my work as ministry and not monotony. Only then will there be joy in the job.

In Your Midst

Shout, and sing for joy, O inhabitant of Zion, for great in your midst is the Holy One of Israel.

—Isaiah 12:6 ESV

Think about your favorite actor, author, or singer. How excited would you be if you bumped into that person at a local coffee shop? Or imagine being a country music fan and ending up just a few pews away from the Oak Ridge Boys during a church outing in Nashville. You might do your best to focus on the choir, but "Elvira" would surely be playing in your head!

It's hard to contain yourself when you're in the presence of someone you've admired for a long time. Now imagine for a moment that God Himself was in your midst. Could you contain yourself if the Creator of the universe was as close as your next breath? Brace yourself, because He is!

Do you have a desire to live more joyfully? Ask God to reveal Himself to you. Once we realize that He is in our midst, we will be singing for joy.

Open my eyes, Lord, so that I can see You all around me, and then I'll sing and shout for joy.

Comfort and Joy

When anxiety was great within me, your consolation brought me joy.

—Psalm 94:19

hink back to your childhood. Was there an item that brought you comfort at bedtime? Perhaps it was a parent or an older sibling. Maybe it was a stuffed animal or a special blanket someone made by hand. Maybe you still have it; more than one person has tossed many years' worth of possessions into a Dumpster while cleaning out the attic but refused to part with Happy Bear or Max the Lion because they want to hang on to fond memories.

Many people spend years searching for ways to ease their anxieties. They may turn to certain people, activities, or substances. The problem is that none of those things bring much consolation, and they certainly don't deliver joy. But when you discover that God eases the ache of anxiety, it will bring you great joy.

Joy comes when we learn where to turn for comfort. Whether at bedtime or in the middle of the day, whenever your anxiety makes itself known, turn to your heavenly Father. In his letter to the Corinthians, Paul described God as the "God of all comfort" (2 Corinthians 1:3). Only He can bring us perfect comfort and joy.

You are the source of comfort and joy for me, God. Thank You for always being there for me and easing the anxieties within me.

The Joy of Making Room

If you have food, share it with those who are hungry.

—Luke 3:11 NLT

The average house in America (even one that most of us would consider just a cottage) is huge by most of the world's standards. Our dinner tables are sprawling, and our idea of a meal is three times the amount of food that most cultures eat in one sitting. Many American families spend the week after Christmas trying to give away leftover cookies and cakes because they can't eat them all. Yet many people will spend this Christmas without shelter, or all alone, or hungry. Some of these people live in your town, perhaps even on your street. They might be a next-door neighbor, a senior from the senior living complex, a college student who can't afford to fly home, or a single man or woman whose family lives far away.

Take a look at your dinner table. Count the extra chairs you keep in the closet. Consider how much food is going to be on your buffet table on Christmas Day. Do you have room for one more?

Lord, I want my family to experience the joy of making room for one more on Christmas Day. Show me who that person is.

Faithful

If we are faithless, he remains faithful, for he cannot disown himself.

—2 Timothy 2:13

Most new Christians seem to be convinced that when they sin, God is angry at and disappointed in them. Some feel they can't ask anything of Him even though they've been forgiven; they think they must "deserve" His love. Perhaps some of this attitude dates back to our Santa Claus days, when we were asked if we had been naughty or nice that year. The implication was that if we had not been on our best behavior, we wouldn't get any presents—at least not any we wanted. In some countries, "Santa" would leave a naughty child nothing but a lump of coal.

God never leaves us a lump of coal. If we confess and repent of our sins, our slates are wiped totally clean; it's as if we never sinned at all. We're declared "Not guilty." God is not disappointed in us. When we are weak or faithless, He remains faithful. The important thing is not that we fell, but that we got up again. Rejoice! Even in our weakest moments, God is faithful!

Lord, like the author of the song "Amazing Grace," I might not understand how You could love a wretch like me, but You do. Praise You and thank You!

A Legacy of Joy

The memory of one who lived with integrity brings joy.
—Proverbs 10:7 VOICE

We're in that season when families travel great distances to reconnect, share long conversations, eat meals, carry out traditions, and reminisce about relatives that the little ones never got to meet. Maybe your grandfather passed away years ago, but he still comes up in every family exchange. Without fail, these conversations involve plenty of laughter and fond memories. Aunts and uncles exchange stories about the time Grandpa fell into the farm pond or hung Grandma's false teeth on the Christmas tree. He's not physically in the room, but he's left a legacy of joy that affects the whole family.

Some people prompt family feuds even after they're gone. Others trigger sorrow, and others spread joy. How do you want to be known? What sort of memories do you want to leave for those you love?

If you'd like to impart joy to your descendants, start today.

Please allow me to teach my family holy joy and devotion to You, Lord. I want to leave a legacy that stretches into eternity.

Joy in Our Liberator

My soul lifts up the Lord! My spirit celebrates God, my Liberator!
—Luke 1:46–47 VOICE

We all need Jesus. No one's exempt. Every human being on planet earth (and all who have gone before us) has a desperate need for the Creator and is hopelessly, eternally lost without Him. The most die-hard atheist—the one who'd never, ever willingly admit to belief in God—is helplessly lost without Him, in spite of his unwavering opinions. The fact that he doesn't believe he needs the God of the Bible doesn't make him any less destitute.

By the same token, the most devout Christian who ever lived was initially just as lost as that die-hard atheist until he or she surrendered to Jesus. Saint Francis, the Reverend Billy Graham, and yes, even Jesus' own mother, Mary—all of them were adrift without Jesus. Mary knew this. In her spirit, she realized as she sang the song recorded in Luke 1 that she'd delivered her own Deliverer, and that realization gave her unspeakable joy.

Hallelujah!

Lord, I was lost, dying, and miserable without You. Thank You for loving, saving, and liberating me.

Above the Enemy

And now my head shall be lifted up above my enemies all around
me, and I will offer in his tent sacrifices with shouts of joy; I will
sing and make melody to the LORD.

—Psalm 27:6 ESV

We live in a world full of bullies. They seem to be every-where, don't they? We can find them on the Internet and on television, and there's still the good old-fashioned schoolyard variety. If you've ever dealt with a bully, you're aware of the stress he or she can cause.

How, then, was the psalmist able to offer shouts of joy even though enemies were "all around" him? David had a history with the Lord, and He had proven to be a faithful protector. David's head had been lifted above his enemies.

As followers of Christ, we have an enemy. He is a bully of the worst kind and would love to steal our joy. We have to remind ourselves that he is already a conquered foe. The Lord has lifted our heads above the enemy, and we can enter the Lord's presence with shouts of joy.

You are greater than the enemy, Lord. Through You, we have the
joy of victory.

Awesome God

Clap your hands, all peoples! Shout to God with loud songs of joy!
—Psalm 47:1 ESV

Think about times you have cheered out loud. Maybe your sports team won a game, your child won an award, or you ran into someone you hadn't seen in a long time. Can you feel a little of the excitement now just thinking about it?

Imagine yourself in a crowd of people listening to the psalmist cry out, "Clap your hands! Shout! Sing loudly!" What would be the reason for such a joyous celebration? God Himself is the reason. God's people should clap, shout, and sing because He, "the Most High, is awe-inspiring" (Psalm 47:2 HCSB).

If it's been a while since you had a clapping, shouting, singing-with-joy kind of moment, remind yourself of the God who lives within you. He is the Creator and Sustainer of life itself. He is responsible for your every breath. He is mightier than all the forces on earth. And He chose you (Psalm 47:4). Let the clapping begin.

You are awesome, Lord, and worthy of celebration. I will clap my hands and shout for joy because of Your love for me.

Joyfully Adventurous

Benaiah . . . performed great exploits. He struck down Moab's two
mightiest warriors. He also went down into a pit on a snowy day
and killed a lion. And he struck down a huge Egyptian. . . . Such
were the exploits of Benaiah son of Jehoiada.

—2 Samuel 23:20–22

Sometimes we lack joy because we refuse to be bold and take a leap of faith into something new and different, no matter how insistently the Lord challenges us to do just that. We like the feeling of security that routine and familiarity bring, even though these things can snuff out joy. Before long we're unhappy and listless.

An adventurous spirit is a gift from God. We're made for exploits! Who was bolder and braver than Jesus Himself?

Many times God leads His children in new directions. But if we decide it's easier to stay put, and we refuse to take the initiative to change our circumstances, we'll miss out on His plans for us. If God is offering you a chance to take a leap of faith for the cause of the kingdom, refuse to give in to fear. Say yes. Determine to step out of your comfort zone and embrace adventure, and then get ready for renewed joy.

Lord, I'll follow You anywhere, including the adventure to which
You've been calling me. Hold my hand as I take this leap of faith!

You Are Loved

Long ago the LORD said to Israel: "I have loved you, my people, with an everlasting love. With unfailing love I have drawn you to myself."

—Jeremiah 31:3 NLT

If we could comprehend and accept who we are in Christ, we would be the most joyful people on the planet. The God of the universe absolutely adores each and every one of us. Too often we look in the mirror and we are critical of what we see. We see every blemish and wrinkle. That is not at all what our God sees!

God loves you with a love that has no limit and no end. He looked through time, desired your presence, and sent His Son to die because He couldn't imagine an eternity without you in it. Doesn't that make your heart jump joyfully?

Are you lacking a little joy today? Perhaps you need to remind yourself that God is looking down from heaven, and He is thrilled that *you* are in His world. You can't help but live joyfully when you realize how much you are loved.

I would be lost without Your love, Lord. Knowing how much You care fills my heart with joy.

Time for a Change

Whoever heeds life-giving correction will be at home among the wise.

—Proverbs 15:31

Have you ever offered someone constructive criticism and then been shocked when that person actually received it with grace and made a change in behavior? Living joyfully is possible only when we're willing to allow the Lord to assess our faults and weaknesses, and then make changes. As this year comes to an end, are you eager for God to reveal your blind spots and help you enter the new year as a healthier, stronger person? If so, read the following statements aloud and pay attention to any that jump out at you:

I like to be in control.

I'm poor at keeping in touch with loved ones.

I'm unlikely to keep confidences.

I can be unapproachable or intimidating.

I'm sometimes difficult to communicate with.

I think I'm always right and am hesitant to consider others' views.

Now, read this one aloud:

Change is good, and I'm eager to improve!

Ask the Lord to help you, and discover the joy that comes from growing in character.

Lord, I want to experience the joy that comes with maturing in the faith and in character. Show me where I'm weak, and then help me to improve.

Joy in Small Changes

Be transformed by the renewing of your mind.

—Romans 12:2

Talking about making some significant changes can be invigorating—but sometimes there's not a whole lot of *doing*. Setting your sights on losing ten pounds, starting that blog, joining the gym, and remodeling the kitchen is great, but what happens four or five weeks later when you realize you haven't completed (or even started!) a single thing on your list? There goes your enthusiasm—and joy.

This year, make sure your list of resolutions isn't very long. Better yet, choose just two or three meaningful goals with the ultimate aim of *consistency in just one*. That's right, following through with just one goal can change the direction of a life. Ask anyone who's ever walked just a few miles—or learned five new foreign words—every week for a year.

Determine to spend just fifteen minutes a day engaged in the activity of your choice and to never miss more than two days per week. You'll find that fifteen minutes will often turn into thirty, or even sixty.

Have a joyful New Year!

Lord, please show me what goal(s) to set in the coming new year, and then help me be consistent and make real changes.

Scripture Index

Scripture Index

Scripture Index

Scripture Index

Scripture Index

Scripture Index

Scripture Index

Scripture Index

Scripture Index

Scripture Index

Scripture Index

Scripture Index

Scripture Index

Scripture Index